CHAT GPT MILLIONAIRE GOLDMINE

UNLOCK THE SECRET TO FINANCIAL SUCCESS AND AI MASTERY BIBLE

AUSTIN WELCH

"ChatGPT Goldmine is not simply a guidebook - it is your ticket into an elite circle of digital marketers and entrepreneurs. Packed with step-by-step instructions, proven strategies, and practical approaches, this book should become your essential partner to guide your journey of turning this tool into your source of revenue and mastering ChatGPT completely. if ChatGPT becomes your main source of income and success. Keep reading to find out how you can take the necessary steps for maximum returns!"

CONTENTS

INTRODUCTION

Introduction

"Imagine living in a digital universe in which every interaction and every word you say represents a golden opportunity, where everything from interactions with clients and colleagues to creating products is gifts that you control like never before."

Artificial intelligence (AI) has revolutionized how we interact, learn, and conduct business at this pivotal juncture in digital history. ChatGPT stands out as one such innovation and promises much more than simply being another chatbot.

Do you remember when you first learned of ChatGPT? Chances are that it left you intrigued, uncertain, and even anxious; all perfectly normal responses. But something inside you must have told you there was hidden potential here that no one has fully explored yet.

Many people experience an initial rush of curiosity, but few manage to understand and exploit the full potential that ChatGPT offers. Feeling as though an opportunity has passed you by without understanding how to take advantage of it is never pleasant.

I understand your frustration at standing on the brink and not knowing how to take that first step forward. But let me assure you: the answers lie within reach! Imagine a world in which your communication turns into revenue; every prompt serves as an invitation for your audience to interact, buy, and trust you - becoming not just another user but a ChatGPT master is within your grasp!

However, becoming a master is more than an idle wish: it requires clear guidance, defined steps, and decisive actions that this book provides you with.

Let me introduce myself. My name is Austin Welch and I'm a digital entrepreneur with extensive experience in digital marketing and online business development, having pioneered innovative approaches over my decade-plus career. Each brand and project that I launched redefines what it means to be an entrepreneur in today's digital era; each idea, product, or launch is part of an evolving chain that has resulted in millions being generated via the Internet; creative analysis is my lifeblood!

My interest in artificial intelligence and ChatGPT quickly evolved into an endless world of potential. From skeptical initial assessments of its practical applicability, to quickly becoming fascinated with its endless capabilities and revenue streams. ChatGPT's ability to generate text in a human-like fashion was revolutionary and has formed the basis of several of my recent successful businesses. Through intensive research and practical application, I now possess an expert-level understanding of this potent tool; knowledge I wish to impart to others so they may also use this potency tool effectively and exponentially increase income streams online.

In the pages of "ChatGPT Goldmine", I will pass on to you not only my knowledge, but also my passion for AI. I have spent countless hours perfecting methods and strategies that take full advantage of ChatGPT's capabilities, transforming digital interactions into tangible results. This book is the compendium of all that: a practical guide infused with the knowledge of an expert, someone who has seen the birth and evolution of this AI, who has directly experienced its transformative impact, and who has been able to capitalize on it to generate more revenue and bring value to thousands of people.

With each chapter, you will not only learn to use ChatGPT but to think like someone who has unlocked the deepest secrets of artificial intelligence to create unparalleled business opportunities. You are about to enter a new universe of possibilities unimaginable before you start reading this book.

This is a journey towards mastering the use of ChatGPT for creating a digital empire, and each chapter is an in-depth exploration of how you can use this powerful tool to your financial advantage.

First, we'll dive into the evolution of natural language processing, highlighting how ChatGPT has revolutionized human-machine interaction and how it stacks up against its competitors in the conversational AI space. I'll show you how economic opportunities are emerging from this breakthrough, and how content can be more than informative: it can be lucrative.

We will discover how numerous brands and companies are transforming what in the past were purely administrative and repetitive tasks through ChatGPT and numerous entrepreneurs are offering these services to companies monetizing the use of AI and generating business that was unimaginable years ago. I will walk you through case studies where ChatGPT conversations have resulted in real revenue and how you can adapt these strategies to connect with your target audience.

Establishing your personal or professional brand using ChatGPT as the central tool is the next step. By exploring niche markets and learning to position your brand effectively, you'll explore how AI-enhanced branding and SEO optimization can elevate visibility while creating a professional digital presence can transform into success in this digital era.

By immersing yourself in the world of communication 2.0, every interaction can become a business opportunity. You will learn to personalize conversations and turn them into sales while increasing conversion rates on digital platforms such as ChatGPT - making every conversation count!

Monetization becomes an art when combined with ethics and security - essential aspects of digital commerce. I will teach you how to balance revenue with integrity while meeting ethical and legal challenges associated with AI monetization to build an authentic brand that's respected among its audience. You will also be shown how to address criticism or controversy professionally while keeping communications transparent and authentic.

Are You Prepared for AI Innovations? This book will equip you to be an early adopter of new technologies and strategies to keep up with digital monetization trends and remain ahead of your game in digital monetization.

This book includes an in-depth directory of AI tools that complement ChatGPT and provides practical instructions on combining them effectively according to your requirements. There are tool evaluations, tips for selecting them, and advice on using them together for superior yet sustainable and scalable results.

With "ChatGPT Goldmine," you will not only learn how to speak the world's most advanced language generation machine; you will also discover ways to make every word and interaction count and every strategy profitable. Don't just look at me; join me on this exciting journey of discovery and mastery and reach unprecedented digital prosperity! Are you ready? The journey begins now - welcome to the future!

CHAPTER 1

HOW CHAT GPT WORKS: FROM ZERO TO ONE GUIDE FOR DUMMIES

ChatGPT stands out in an ever-evolving world of artificial intelligence as an oasis of hope and possibility. However, for those unfamiliar with it, ChatGPT may seem daunting and intimidating - don't despair though, this guide is here to unlock its power even if you are starting from scratch!

What is ChatGPT?

ChatGPT, developed by OpenAI, is a variant of the GPT (Generative Pre-trained Transformer) language model. It's designed to generate human-like text based on the input it receives. This AI tool can write essays, create code, answer questions, and even mimic conversation, making it an incredibly versatile tool for various applications.

How Does ChatGPT Work?

At its core, ChatGPT employs a deep learning algorithm called a transformer to analyze massive text data sets and predict which words belong in subsequent sentences. Over time, the transformer becomes adept at producing coherent and contextually appropriate texts when given prompts from a user.

Getting Started with ChatGPT

1. Accessing ChatGPT: To start using ChatGPT, you can access it through platforms that host the AI, like the OpenAI website. Some platforms might require you to create an account or subscribe to use the service.

2. Understanding the Interface: Once you access ChatGPT, you'll typically find a text box where you can type your prompts or questions. The AI will respond in a conversational format.

3. Crafting Effective Prompts: The key to leveraging ChatGPT is in how you frame your prompts. Be clear and specific about what you want. For example, instead of saying, "Tell me about dogs," try "What are the main care needs for Labrador Retrievers?"

Practical Uses of ChatGPT

1. Content Creation: ChatGPT can help you write articles, blogs, scripts, and even creative stories. Provide it with a topic and some key points, and let it generate a draft for you.

2. Coding Assistance: For those in software development, ChatGPT can write code snippets and help debug existing code.

3. Learning and Research: ChatGPT can summarize complex topics, answer questions, and provide explanations, making it a powerful tool for students and professionals alike.

4. Language Translation: While not a replacement for professional translation services, ChatGPT can assist in translating text between languages.

ChatGPT and The Art of Prompt Engineering

Effective communication with ChatGPT is key to realizing its full potential, and prompt engineering (the art and science of creating prompts) is both art and science. We will discuss its nuances while offering concrete examples to guide you.

Basics of Prompt Engineering

Prompt engineering involves creating input to ChatGPT that yields the most useful and accurate response from its users. The quality of output you obtain from ChatGPT relies heavily on how well-phrased your prompt is.

Crafting Effective Prompts

- **Be Specific**: The more specific your prompt, the more tailored the response. Instead of asking "How can I cook rice?", try asking instead "What is the recipe for making Basmati rice for two people?"
- **Provide Context**: If your query is part of a larger task or question, provide that context. For instance, "As part of a healthy weight loss diet, what are some low-calorie ways to prepare chicken breast?"
- **Sequence Your Questions**: If you have multiple questions, start with a broad query and then narrow down. Begin with, "What is Python used for in programming?" and follow up with, "Can you provide an example of a simple Python script for data analysis?"

Examples of ChatGPT Prompts

- **For Content Creation**: "Write a blog intro about the impact of AI on digital marketing trends in 2023."

- **For Coding Help**: "I'm trying to merge two lists in Python without duplicates. Here's my current code: [insert code]. How can I improve it?"
- **For Language Learning**: "Provide a dialogue between two friends meeting in a cafe in Spanish, including greetings, ordering food, and saying goodbye."
- **For Research**: "Summarize the key points from the latest research on renewable energy sources."

Refining and Building on Responses

Sometimes the first response from ChatGPT might not fully meet your needs. Don't hesitate to refine your prompt or ask follow-up questions. For instance, if the initial recipe for Basmati rice isn't what you expected, you could follow up with, "Can you provide a simpler version of the Basmati rice recipe for beginners?"

Advanced Tips for Using ChatGPT

1. **Prompt Engineering**: This involves crafting prompts that guide ChatGPT to produce more accurate and relevant responses. Experiment with different styles and structures of prompts.
2. **Fine-tuning Responses**: You can guide ChatGPT to refine its responses. If the initial answer isn't quite right, follow up with more specific questions or directions.
3. **Combining Outputs**: Sometimes, the best result comes from combining multiple responses from ChatGPT. Use its outputs as building blocks for your projects.

Mastering Response Styles in ChatGPT

Getting the most out of ChatGPT isn't just about asking the right questions; it's also about guiding how you want those questions answered. This involves understanding and utilizing different response styles. Let's delve into various ways you can instruct ChatGPT to respond, enhancing the effectiveness of your interactions.

Requesting Summaries

If you're looking for concise information, direct ChatGPT to summarize the content. For example, "Summarize the main points of the latest IPCC report on climate change."

Imagining Scenarios

For creative or hypothetical situations, use prompts like, "Imagine a scenario where renewable energy has completely replaced fossil fuels. Describe a typical day in this world."

3. Creating Tables and Schemas

When you need information in a structured format, ask ChatGPT to organize it into a table or schema. For instance, "Create a table comparing the features, pros, and cons of electric cars versus gasoline cars."

4. Detailed Descriptions

For a deeper understanding of a concept or process, request a detailed description. Try, "Describe in detail how photosynthesis works in plants."

5. 'Act as' Prompts

These prompts are powerful for role-playing or simulating specific characters or experts. Say, "Act as a fitness coach and provide a one-week workout plan for beginners."

6. Generating Step-by-Step Guides

This is particularly useful for tutorials or processes. You might ask, "Provide a step-by-step guide on how to start a small online business."

7. Crafting Dialogue

For language learning or scriptwriting, use prompts like, "Write a dialogue between two friends planning a vacation, focusing on their budget and destination choices."

8. Creative Compositions

Unleash ChatGPT's creative potential with prompts like, "Compose a short poem about the ocean during sunset."

Conclusion on Response Styles

Mastering these various prompts and response styles allows you to tailor ChatGPT to suit your exact needs, whether for learning, creativity, organization, or entertainment. Remember: the key lies in how you ask. Refining prompts so they accurately reflect not only what information is desired but how it should be presented opens up an abundance of options with ChatGPT - with these techniques you are already well on your way towards becoming a ChatGPT prompt expert capable of drawing out optimal responses in any circumstance.

CHAPTER 2

UNLOCKING THE PROFIT POTENTIAL OF CHATGPT

Silicon Valley was alive with activity when Emma entered a bright conference room filled with lively discussions and clicking keyboards - the backdrop to which was the announcement for today's event: The Age of AI: Unlocking Revenue Opportunities with ChatGPT. Among those present was Emma, a young entrepreneur with big ideas and her laptop filled with dreams.

Emma founded a startup focused on improving customer interaction through emerging technologies, yet hadn't managed to turn her ambition into a sustainable revenue stream - until now! That was about to change.

At first, Emma found the conference rather uninspiring, as the presenters described the early days of natural language processing to modern AIs that can converse, compose poetry, and even code. But soon enough, Emma was riveted as they detailed how ChatGPT had evolved from an open-source project into a powerful digital transformation tool - with no small amount of intrigue about how much change had occurred over time.

Emma eagerly took notes as the presenters discussed strategies for turning communication and content into tangible revenue. From incorporating chatbots into customer service to producing interactive online platform content, they shared numerous monetization strategies which allowed Emma to understand that digital content can not only serve as a channel to connect with customers but also generate direct and indirect revenues when used correctly.

Lucas took center stage. Lucas, a freelance writer who had revolutionized his career using ChatGPT, began creating interactive novels where readers could choose the direction of the plot and, as a result, saw amazing results - not only increasing his reader base but also finding new revenue streams through subscriptions and custom content creation.

Inspired by the possibilities, Emma began to imagine how she could apply these ideas to her own business. She thought about her ideal client, small businesses struggling to keep up with customer service demands, and how a personalized AI service could revolutionize their operations and their day-to-day lives.

Discussion then ensued surrounding ChatGPT as an effective means to enhance customer experiences. Examples were shared of major brands that had successfully used ChatGPT to deliver personalized product recommendations tailored specifically to each user, helping customers make more informed purchasing decisions and increasing both sales and satisfaction levels.

Emma realized how, with each new story and case study, ChatGPT could fit together the pieces of her business vision. ChatGPT provided not only automated answers to frequently asked questions (FAQs) but also collected key customer data that further tailored customer experiences.

The last chapter of the conference served as a rallying cry to constantly innovate and evolve, emphasizing not becoming complacent with current AI applications but instead finding new uses for them in creating value.

Emma took time to reflect upon all she had learned at ChatGPT, having come in search of inspiration but leaving with so much more. With ideas swirling through her head and excitement pulsing through her veins, she knew she had discovered something truly great; her journey towards financial independence and entrepreneurial success through ChatGPT had just begun; now was the time for action!

Emma felt powerless as the conference room slowly filled with enthusiasts discussing AI. While excitement abounded at its potential to enhance her business vision, Emma felt as if something were keeping her still; rather it was realizing she and her small business were part of an online revolution that could alter human interaction and revenue generation in profound ways.

Emma picked up her notebook with both determination and anxiety for what lay ahead, sketching how ChatGPT could fit into her business model and personalizing customer experiences - from creating virtual assistants who provided tailored advice to customer interfaces that learned with every interaction. Emma knew this journey would not be easy or smooth sailing;

She imagined a service where ChatGPT could not only answer customer inquiries but also anticipate customer needs - offering solutions even before customers knew they had issues. ChatGPT could manage inventories, provide technical support, cross-sell products, and assist in after-sales management all within one seamless dialogue session.

Emma knew the key to ChatGPT's success wasn't just its technology; rather it lay in how she presented it and told its story. To achieve maximum effectiveness she must create an experience for customers that makes them feel understood and cared for on an intimate level.

With that story in mind, Emma considered various monetization strategies. How could she turn this advanced service into a steady revenue source? Subscriptions seemed like the ideal fit, providing different levels of customization while offering steady returns over time. There were also indirect monetization opportunities such as collecting and analyzing customer data for companies who could leverage its benefits.

Emma quickly recognized that adaptability was crucial. With digital technologies constantly shifting and evolving, her business model would need to be flexible enough to quickly pivot with changing trends and technologies.

Just then, as though in answer to his thoughts, his phone vibrated: an email from an investor acquaintance who had attended the conference and been impressed by Emma's passion and vision during a short conversation during a break; they wanted to meet and explore how they could work together to bring her vision to market.

Emma closed her notebook as her mind raced with possibilities she hadn't anticipated. As she stood up, feeling almost light-footed for once, Emma knew this opportunity had finally arrived - not only through its speakers' words but also in human connection and potential future partnerships.

She knew the road ahead would be filled with challenges, yet was full of optimism for transforming not only her own business but also how businesses and customers communicated. ChatGPT would become her ally in accomplishing her vision.

Emma left the conference room feeling full of gratitude for an event that had been more than informative; it had been transformative. And at that moment, Emma and ChatGPT's story had only just begun.

With the promise of meeting an investor ringing in her head, Emma navigated the busy streets with renewed purpose. Each step seemed to move her one step closer to not only her future business but also some greater goal; ChatGPT wasn't just another tool - it opened a whole new world of human interactions enhanced by technology.

Over the subsequent weeks, Emma immersed herself in studying ChatGPT and conversational AI capabilities. Her focus was to understand how automated interactions could appear so natural to customers that they wouldn't even notice the difference; thus she tested prototypes, tweaked responses accordingly, and monitored conversations for any issues with communication flow.

As his knowledge of technology expanded, so did his vision for his company. He imagined offering services where every customer felt unique and appreciated - where ChatGPT could act not only as a facilitator but also as an integral link in developing customer-business relationships at levels never seen before.

Emma was making progress toward creating the story she desired with her business. Instead of selling products, Emma focused on creating experiences where AI and humanity worked hand in hand to increase customer satisfaction and loyalty to unprecedented levels.

Emma met with her investor quickly. In a trendy cafe filled with chatter and the sound of coffee cups being clinked together, Emma explained her vision - including using ChatGPT in customer service, personalization at scale, and collecting data to further improve user experiences.

"Your vision goes beyond monetization," the investor observed with admiration, "and you want to create an ecosystem where technology and human touch not only coexist but augment each other."

Armed with financial support in place, Emma set about creating her platform. She recruited a team of developers and designers - each contributing a unique set of talents - who together developed ChatGPT as the engine behind their creation of an almost magical system that handled interactions effortlessly and gracefully.

Soon, early user testing began to show promising results. Users were impressed with ChatGPT's speed and accuracy in responding. What particularly amazed Emma was how many users seemed to connect emotionally with it; many interacted with ChatGPT not just out of necessity but voluntarily as well.

Emma's company soon garnered significant acclaim. Articles appeared on technology and business blogs, she was invited to speak at conferences, and an article appeared in an established business magazine with headlines like: "The Humanization of AI". One journalist highlighted Emma's unique blend of narrative and technology to produce something truly exceptional.

Emma never lost sight of the core story as her company expanded. Each update and upgrade she implemented reflected her desire to make each interaction meaningful, giving customers something they could take with them as part of a memorable customer experience.

Although technology would continue advancing at an exponential pace, Emma knew this marked just the start of a new era where humanity and artificial intelligence joined forces - with herself at its helm leading this new chapter of history.

Emma and her team worked to perfect their platform over several months. As time passed, their story and that of their customers became ever more interwoven; one filled with innovation and discovery - ChatGPT had become the silent protagonist here, an ever-present ally ready to learn, adapt, and anticipate user needs.

But with growth came new challenges. New competitors emerged, trying to emulate what Emma had created while others offered unique conversational AI approaches. For Emma to remain relevant and connect with her audience effectively, more was required than advanced technology: she needed a narrative that resonated on an individual basis with every customer.

He launched a campaign to collect user stories demonstrating how ChatGPT had positively impacted their lives in small but significant ways. One mother found relief balancing work and family thanks to AI-powered customer service; an entrepreneur saved her startup from logistical difficulty through quick interactions with virtual assistants; while a student found comfort and support in late-night discussions as she worked through exam stress.

Emma used these human stories as the cornerstone of her brand, ChatGPT. Each testimonial proved its promise of understanding, supporting, and amplifying human capabilities.

As Emma's company was nominated for an illustrious technology innovation award, the awards ceremony brought together some of the brightest minds from both technology and business to celebrate achievements and look ahead.

As soon as Emma heard that her company had won, Emma took to the stage with her team. In an emotional speech that focused on humanizing code and providing empathy-inducing automated interactions while acknowledging the vibrant community surrounding their platform.

"This award," he stated with a smile, "isn't just for our technology; it recognizes all the stories we've helped tell, lives we have touched, and the future we are working towards together."

An enthusiastic reception greeted Emma's tale that night. Not only had she built an effective business but had also shown how artificial intelligence combined with storytelling can enrich our lives in unimaginable ways.

As she and her team left the stage lights dimmed and applause faded away, Emma knew her story with ChatGPT was far from over; rather it marked just the start of an exciting chapter at the intersection of technology and humanity that they would continue to craft with every innovation, interaction, and life touched by ChatGPT users.

As she basked in her success and applause echoed around her, Emma reflected on the path that had led to this momentous moment in time. While the awards ceremony marked the end of one chapter, it also heralded an entirely new phase with lessons and opportunities ahead; her success story would serve as an inspirational tale for others who hoped to replicate it.

Emma felt inspired after accomplishing so much; with a fresh perspective and renewed energy, she began the following day to draft what would become a handbook for future ChatGPT users: "Unlocking the Lucrative Potential of ChatGPT," an apt tribute to both her journey and those following in it.

Introduction. His introduction provided a history of natural language processing and ChatGPT's transformative effects on the digital market landscape, opening new economic opportunities. He recounted stories of competitors and collaborators alike to emphasize how technology and human storytelling were merging to create an entirely new playing field where empathy met artificial intelligence.

Emma used straightforward yet captivating language to explain how communication and content could become tangible revenue streams. Instead of only discussing abstract theories, Emma provided real-life case studies and testimonials from individuals whose lives had been transformed by ChatGPT; entrepreneurs, freelancers, and even large corporations found this tool an effective way of improving customer experience and increasing sales.

Emma went beyond providing examples and strategies; her writing included an invitation to view ChatGPT as more than just a tool. According to Emma, its true magic lay in merging the analytical power of AI with the warmth and complexity of human storytelling - an approach which was the basis for ChatGPT's incredible success and proved the point she made about its transformational nature.

"Technology," wrote Mr. Sobeloff, "is only as powerful as the stories it allows us to share. ChatGPT serves as a writing instrument; how we choose to use it may have profound effects on human lives. Financial freedom may be desirable but true freedom lies in charting our course and sharing our tales."

Emma realized she had created something truly exceptional when she received a draft chapter for ChatGPT's draft chapter in her hands. Not only had she captured its practical applications and the human aspect behind its code, she had also created an invaluable resource not just for entrepreneurs seeking financial freedom but for all people looking to understand how technology could enrich their lives as well as those around them.

Thus, Emma's chapter served not only as a lesson in monetization and business strategy, but also as an invitation to embrace the digital age with humanity and purpose. And as she submitted her manuscript for publication, she felt confident that her story and guidance would inspire others to write their own chapters of success in the dynamic and ever-evolving world of artificial intelligence.

With the manuscript ready to send, Emma sat in her study, contemplating the soft glow of dawn. Her mind danced with ideas, each a glimmer of what the future might hold for her readers. She wondered if they would be as eager and ready to take the leap as she had been.

The "click" of his email sent marked a turning point. It was a bridge between his story and that of countless others who, perhaps, would find in his words the spark to ignite their own fires of innovation.

The days went by and soon the responses began to come in. They were not only from grateful readers but from real people who had applied its teachings and were already seeing changes in their lives. There were stories of small business owners who, using ChatGPT, had redefined their customer service and expanded their markets. There were also stories of freelancers who had found in AI a way to improve their efficiency and creativity, and thus, their income.

Emma decided to go the extra mile and host a webinar, inviting those who had used her chapter as a stepping stone for their entrepreneurial ventures. The virtual room filled up quickly, and the screens glowed with faces from around the world, each one illuminated by the promise of the digital age.

The session was more than a lecture; it became a weaving of narratives, with Emma at the core, facilitating a conversation that was more a tapestry of experiences than a one-way lesson. They shared successes and failures, laughs and learnings. The energy was palpable, even across digital connections.

Emma listened to each story, each unique ChatGPT application, and knew that her chapter had transcended its pages. It had become a community, a network of minds thinking beyond the boundaries of their circumstances, united by the will to shape the future.

At the end of the seminar, a young entrepreneur asked, "What's the next chapter, Emma? What comes after this beginning?"

She smiled, knowing the answer lay in each of them. "The next chapter is written by you," she said. "I simply gave you some guidelines and shared my story. But each of you is living your own journey with ChatGPT. Share it, as I shared mine, and together, let's build something we can't even imagine yet."

With that conclusion, Emma closed the session, but the dialogue that had begun was just warming up. Participants continued the conversation in online forums, chat groups and virtual meetings, expanding the legacy of that first chapter.

In the weeks and months that followed, "ChatGPT Goldmine" not only became a best-seller, but a catalyst for a vibrant and collaborative community. Emma continued to write, educate and connect. And although she was considered a trailblazer, she knew that her true success lay in the successes of those she had inspired.

For beyond strategies and revenue, Emma had embedded in her work a deeper truth: that at the heart of the digital age, where artificial intelligence and humanity meet, lies a limitless potential not only to create wealth, but to enrich lives.

And so, as Emma's story intertwined with those of others, her opening chapter became the prologue to many stories yet to be told, each reflecting the light of possibility she had kindled.

As Emma's words resonated in the collective consciousness of her audience, the impetus for practical action grew. Her story had ignited a spark, but to keep the flame alive, it was essential to return to the theoretical and practical foundations that formed the basis of her teaching.

Emma then decided to organize a series of hands-on workshops to complement the inspirational narrative with robust theory and applicability. The next workshop was entitled "Unlocking the Lucrative Potential of ChatGPT: From Theory to Practice".

Session 1: Introduction to the ChatGPT Universe

He began with a review of the history and evolution of natural language processing (NLP), showing how natural language interfaces had evolved from simple grammatical rules to sophisticated predictive models based on vast data sets. He explained how NLP had reached a tipping point with the introduction of ChatGPT, which not only understood and generated text, but could also learn from interaction and improve over time.

Session 2: Turning Communication and Content into Tangible Revenue

Here, Emma presented how AI monetization is not an abstract concept, but a tangible reality. She presented direct monetization models, such as paid content creation or premium virtual assistance services, and indirect monetization, through improved customer service or process optimization that can lead to higher sales and lower operating expenses.

Session 3: Case Studies and Monetization Strategies

To illustrate these points, he shared case studies of individuals and companies that had applied these theories. For example, a freelance writer who used ChatGPT to generate article outlines, or a small business that implemented a chatbot to handle after-hours customer inquiries, thereby increasing their leads and conversions.

Session 4: Tailoring Strategies for Target Audiences

The workshop also addressed the importance of adapting technology and monetization strategies to the target audience. Emma stressed that understanding the audience is key, as the same tool can be applied in multiple ways depending on the needs and behaviors of the market.

Session 5: Improving Customer Experience with ChatGPT

Finally, he emphasized how ChatGPT can be a valuable tool for improving the customer experience. Practical examples included customer service chatbots that learn and adapt to frequently asked questions, and personalized recommendation systems that can increase conversion rates and build customer loyalty.

The combination of inspirational storytelling and practical teaching resonated with the audience. It was no longer just the success stories of others that motivated them, but also the clear understanding of how they could apply those same principles to their unique circumstances.

In closing the workshop, Emma reminded her participants that theory without action is sterile, but action without understanding is blind. She invited each attendee to become a storyteller in their own right, not only sharing their success, but also the processes and theory behind them.

In the end, what began as the story of a single person became a symphony of voices, all sharing the same vision: to use artificial intelligence not as an end, but as a means to create a more prosperous and fulfilling future for all.

With the theoretical foundations firmly established, Emma opened the floor for questions and interactive dialogues. She knew that true understanding came from discussion and application of knowledge. The group was diverse: some were AI novices, others had deeper technical knowledge, but all shared the common goal of turning ChatGPT into a revenue stream.

Practical Interlude: Questions and Answers

One after another, the participants began to ask questions:

- "How can we ensure that AI-generated content is unique and valuable?"
- "Which monetization strategies are the most sustainable in the long term?"
- "How can we measure the impact of ChatGPT on customer experience?"

Emma responded with patience and clarity, using real examples to illustrate her point. She explained the importance of combining human creativity with ChatGPT efficiency to create unique content. She talked about revenue diversification and adaptability as keys to sustainable monetization. And he highlighted customer satisfaction and conversion metrics as indicators of ChatGPT's impact.

Practical Exercise Session

The workshop culminated with a series of hands-on exercises where attendees could outline their monetization plans using ChatGPT. They worked in groups, encouraging collaboration and peer-to-peer learning. Emma and her team moved among the groups, providing guidance and clarification.

For some, the strategy was to create a blog that used ChatGPT to generate draft content. For others, it was to design an enhanced customer service that could scale without significant investment in human resources. And there were those exploring the development of AI-driven educational products for their niche market.

Conclusion and Call to Action

At the conclusion of the workshop, Emma made sure to reinforce the didactic intent of chapter 1 of her book. She summarized the key lessons and how each could be applied in the real world. But more importantly, she urged each participant to take concrete action.

- "Identify a need in your market that ChatGPT can fill," he suggested.
- "Experiment with small projects before scaling up."
- "Use feedback to iterate and improve your offerings."

It reminded them that the digital marketplace is vast and constantly changing, and that adaptability and continuous learning are crucial. ChatGPT was a powerful tool, but like any tool, its value was determined by the skill and creativity of the user.

With a blend of sound theory and practical application, Emma had designed a learning experience that not only educated but also motivated. And with every story shared, every question answered and every plan outlined, participants moved one step closer to turning ChatGPT's lucrative potential into a tangible reality.

As they said goodbye, Emma knew she had started more than just a series of workshops. She had ignited a community of innovators and entrepreneurs who saw ChatGPT not as a fad, but as a fellow traveler in their quest for financial freedom and success. Their story had been the spark, but now, each of them had their own flame to carry forward and share.

CHAPTER 3

BUILD YOUR DIGITAL GOLD MINE WITH CHATGPT

Excitement was palpable as Emma opened up the second session, where participants had emerged brimming with ideas and plans from the initial one. Now was the time to transform those rough diamonds into polished gems.

Home: Establishing the Foundation

Emma began with a quote that always resonated with her, "Digital mining is not just digging in cyberspace; it's building the tools, defining the work area, and knowing where to dig."

- "Identifying your niche," he began, "is like selecting the right place to dig. You don't want to waste your efforts digging in a place with no gold." The room nodded in agreement.

She explained how ChatGPT could be a partner in exploring and analyzing niches, generating content and dialoguing with potential customers to uncover unmet needs.

Development: Branding and Visibility

The importance of branding came next. "In the digital age, your brand is your banner," Emma stated, showing examples of successful brands and how ChatGPT helped create cohesive and engaging brand narratives.

Next, Emma touched on SEO. "Imagine ChatGPT is your modern-day pick and shovel," she said with a smile. "It can help you find the keywords that are the 'golden veins' in the vast world of SEO."

Strategy: Digital Presence and Collaborations

Moving to digital presence was a natural shift. Emma illustrated how a consistent digital presence was essential and how AI could maintain that consistency across multiple platforms.

Collaborations were also key. "Connecting with influencers is like joining forces with other miners to find more gold," he explained. ChatGPT could identify the right influencers and even help draft messages for collaborations.

Theory to Practice: Authority and Leadership

Becoming an authority was the next step. "Content is your currency in the digital economy," explained Emma, explaining how ChatGPT could provide users with articles, posts and reports that would establish them as thought leaders in their fields of interest.

He spoke of the strength of content marketing and how ChatGPT enabled it by enabling the production of high quality, volumetric content at an unimaginable speed and consistency.

Trust and Relationships: The Human Touch

Marketing was not just about visibility, it was about trust. Social proof and testimonials could be generated and enhanced with the help of ChatGPT, as long as a core of authenticity was maintained.

"Building strong, long-lasting relationships with your audience is like taking care of your mine," Emma said. "It's not just extracting the gold, but keeping the mine stable and thriving." ChatGPT could analyze market trends and preferences, allowing users to adjust their customer relationship strategies effectively.

Conclusion: More than a Tool, a Partner

"ChatGPT is more than a tool; it is our partner on this journey towards financial independence," Emma asserted with a strong and enthusiastic tone that conveyed her belief in technology's potential.

Participants dispersed, discussing various scenarios. With Emma's guidance, they felt ready and empowered to bring their digital gold into reality.

Emma took time to reflect in silence on their journey together. These chapters were not simply pieces of literature or workshops; rather, they represented chapters of each participant's lives which, thanks to ChatGPT, promised success and achievement.

Emma observed how each person now had some knowledge, yet the real reward would come from their effort and persistence. Returning to her desk, Emma began planning the next stage in their mentees' journey: shifting from theory to practice.

Elaboration of the Treasure Map

"Marketing strategies," he began, "are like your treasure map. You must understand every curve and every mark if you hope to find the richness you seek." Emma knew that in this digital world, strategies were not static; they were dynamic, growing and evolving with every interaction and every piece of content.

With the help of ChatGPT, one could map not only current trends but also predict future ones. AI was like a digital marketing oracle, one that was constantly learning and adapting.

Precision Mining: SEO and Content Analysis

He then turned to SEO: "SEO can be a minefield," he noted wryly, but with ChatGPT you could avoid its traps and find safe routes towards your targets. ChatGPT allowed users to optimize content by tailoring it directly for search algorithms, thus creating pieces of writing which resonated equally well with human audiences and search engines alike.

Emma demonstrated how ChatGPT could analyze competing content to help their users identify which topics had become oversaturated or still had room for fresh perspectives.

Building the Refinery: Quality over Quantity

Quality content was a pillar Emma emphasized. "It's not enough to simply produce. You must refine your content like a precious metal," she advised. ChatGPT wasn't just a content generator; it was a collaborator in the editing process, ensuring that every word published was valuable.

Emma used ChatGPT live to demonstrate how to enhance a simple blog post into a thought-leading piece, adjusting tone, style and complexity to suit the target market.

The Market: Understanding and Adapting

The last part of the session was dedicated to the market. "The market is your river," he compared. "And its current is constantly changing. If you don't adapt, it will sweep you away." Emma highlighted how ChatGPT could be an invaluable market analyst, collecting data from user interactions and providing insights into consumer preferences.

He ended the session with an assignment: each participant was to use ChatGPT to create a content plan and SEO strategy for their particular niche, using the tools and techniques they had learned.

The Story Continues

As the days passed and the story of Emma and her students unfolded, each of them began to see tangible results. Personal brands began to emerge, blogs came to life with relevant content, and product pages were optimized to top search engine rankings.

With each success, confidence grew. ChatGPT was not just a chapter in their careers; it was becoming the storyteller, helping them write their future.

Emma's story was not just one of teaching, but of constant learning. As her students explored and expanded their horizons, she also discovered new ways to apply artificial intelligence in the world of digital marketing.

Closing: The Innovation Narrative

As dusk fell over the room, Emma felt proud and accomplished. Her students' stories demonstrated the power of adaptation and innovation.

"Your story's not yet over," he reminded his mentees. "Every day brings new words into play - so make them unforgettable!"

Emma realized this was only the start. Digital mining was much more than digging for riches - it was about uncovering human ingenuity powered by artificial intelligence and uncovering connections among information systems.

Emma's story, though fictional, captures the spirit of continuous learning and adaptation that every aspiring digital entrepreneur must cultivate. When closing her seminar for the day, Emma reminded her students that every effort they made was an investment in themselves and their professional futures.

Conclusion of Chapter 2: The Treasure of Innovation

Emma told them, "the real treasure lies not in immediate results of their efforts but rather in how these innovative tools transform their experience of digital media - turning information into gold!"

Emma stressed the significance of authenticity and originality when teaching digital content creation, with ChatGPT helping her students craft unique value that resonated with their target audiences and build engagement through authentic online presences that not only drew followers but also fostered loyalty and trust among them.

At the end of each day, Emma's class would disperse, equipped with knowledge and tools for building their digital empires. Some might stay behind late into the night to implement their plans while others reflected upon lessons learned before beginning new tasks.

Emma's experience encapsulated the journey that any digital entrepreneur must embark upon: from theory and practice, learning and teaching, exploring AI's capabilities and applying them in ways that convert communication and content into tangible revenue streams.

Each student would find his/her journey different, yet all shared the same destination: creating their digital goldmine through ChatGPT and Emma's techniques and strategies. Every word written and strategy implemented took them one step closer towards long-awaited financial freedom.

Emma's students embark upon their respective journeys, while this chapter is also an invitation for readers to apply the lessons to their own digital journeys and create revenue or establish meaningful brands through expert guidance and tools available today. With proper tools and guidance in place, the potential of digital era business growth is limitless.

CHAPTER 4

COMMUNICATION 2.0: MORE THAN WORDS, IT'S REVENUE

The Dawn of a New Era

Lucas, an energetic entrepreneur from a vibrant office overlooking a busy cityscape, was considering all the exciting prospects opening before him. After avidly following Emma's course for several months now, he was eager to launch into digital communication revolutionized by artificial intelligence.

Lucas understood the power of words. With ChatGPT at his side, he knew every email, customer service chat, and product description could become an opportunity to connect, persuade and convert viewers into loyal customers. Lucas knew they'd reach unprecedented levels of communication via this tool.

Transforming Every Interaction into a Business Opportunity

a) Personalized Conversations

It started with a focus on personalized conversations. Lucas understood that the era of generic responses and soulless interactions had passed. He configured ChatGPT to analyze the tone, context and preferences of his customers, allowing him to deliver a highly personalized user experience. Every question, every concern, and every comment became an opportunity to strengthen the customer relationship.

b) Strategies to Increase Conversion Rate

Lucas also realized that conversion was not a moment, but a process. He implemented strategies that allowed ChatGPT to guide customers through their sales funnel with a mix of natural conversation and data-driven recommendations. Conversion rates began to climb, and every interaction now seemed like a seed planted in fertile soil.

c) ChatGPT as Sales Assistant

Next, Lucas put ChatGPT at the center of his sales process. He configured the system to act as an assistant that not only answered questions but also made proactive suggestions based on the customer's purchase and browsing history. It was like having a sales team working 24/7, never losing heart or efficiency.

d) Use of Predictive Analytics

With the help of ChatGPT and its predictive analytics capabilities, Lucas was able to stay ahead of its customers' needs. The AI reviewed buying patterns and market trends, anticipating what customers would want before they knew it themselves.

e) Tools and Plugins for E-commerce

Lucas knew that integration was key. He integrated ChatGPT into his e-commerce platform using advanced tools and plugins that allowed for a seamless user experience. From navigation to checkout, the AI was there to assist.

Customer Loyalty and Retention Through AI-Driven Content

a) CRM Systems Driven by ChatGPT

It not only wanted to attract customers but to keep them. That's why it implemented CRM systems powered by ChatGPT that allowed it to maintain constant and relevant communication with its customers. Every message was value-laden, personalized, and timely.

b) Retention Strategies

From newsletters to personalized offers, it used ChatGPT to ensure that every communication strengthened customer loyalty. Retention programs became more sophisticated and effective, keeping the customer base engaged and active.

c) Reduction of Cart Abandonment Rate

Cart abandonment was a problem Lucas had faced before, but with ChatGPT, he found solutions. He implemented automatic reminders, product suggestions based on browsing behavior, and real-time chats to resolve queries at critical moment, which significantly decreased the abandonment rate.

d) Surveys and AI-driven Feedback

Lucas used ChatGPT to send out surveys and solicit feedback, ensuring that every customer's voice was heard and every response informed improvements in service and user experience. This constant feedback became the driver of a continuous improvement process.

e) Loyalty and ChatGPT Programs

Finally, Lucas integrated ChatGPT into its loyalty programs. Members received personalized recommendations, and the AI analyzed reward redemption patterns to optimize offers and increase customer satisfaction.

Revenue Impact

Thanks to the strategic implementation of ChatGPT, Lucas saw exponential growth in revenue. Every interaction had become a sales opportunity, and every customer felt valued and understood. Lucas had not only built a brand, but had created an unforgettable experience for their customers, all thanks to artificial intelligence and communication 2.0.

Lucas' story, paralleling Emma's, showed a universal truth in modern digital business: tools like ChatGPT are not just technology add-ons; they are strategic partners that can transform communication into a solid bridge to financial success.

Lucas was beginning to see the potential of his new venture, thanks to the innovative ChatGPT applications he had successfully integrated into his e-commerce platform. But he knew he was just skimming the surface. He had transformed every customer interaction into a business opportunity, and now he was ready to delve deeper into the strategies that would cement him as a leader in his niche.

Personalized Conversations: From Simple Small Talk to Closing Sales

Lucas implemented a personalized ChatGPT system which not only answered customers' inquiries but also provided tailored recommendations based on past interactions and AI-derived data analysis. This enabled his website visitors to become engaged customers who ultimately made purchases from his business.

Lucas understood the key to success lay in the details. He carefully examined transcripts of ChatGPT interactions to understand common sticking points and objections, then used this knowledge to train his virtual assistant, making her more adept at handling objections and leading customers toward purchase completion.

ChatGPT had evolved beyond being simply a customer service assistant to become an active sales assistant that recognized customer needs before they themselves did; using AI predictive analytics tools it offered additional products or services that complimented past purchases or browsing patterns.

Sustained Growth

Lucas became more adept at applying these strategies, his business saw tremendous growth. Not only was his conversion rate increased significantly; but also, he built up an expanded customer base that saw his brand not just as an easy sale but as an advisor they could trust.

As Lucas' story unfolds, it demonstrates how technology and customization can catapult a company to the forefront of its industry. Furthermore, this chapter could explore how he handles specific challenges while applying lessons learned from every success and failure to continuously enhance his business.

Lucas' story hasn't finished unfolding just yet. To truly understand his journey and the ways Chat GPT integrates with his business strategy, we need to look closely at how customer loyalty and retention principles translate to everyday practices that support his digital venture's long-term expansion.

Maximizing the Potential of Feedback

Lucas realized that customer feedback was a gold mine for continuous improvement. He implemented a post-interaction survey system, which dynamically adjusted to customer responses. This information was converted into concrete actions to improve their products and user experience.

Refining Customer Focus

With each analysis and adjustment, ChatGPT became increasingly attuned to the wants and needs of Lucas' customers. It became an invaluable strategic decision support tool, providing a service that not only answered customers' questions, but anticipated and resolved their concerns before they became barriers to purchase.

Implementing a Revolutionary Loyalty Program

Lucas knew that a loyalty program had to reward not only purchases, but also customer interaction and engagement with the brand. Using AI, he designed a points system that rewarded everything from product reviews to survey participation and social media interaction. This strategy dramatically increased customer retention and turned casual shoppers into brand ambassadors.

Innovating in Customer Service

In addition, Lucas employed ChatGPT to provide 24/7 customer service, exceeding expectations for service and availability. This constant access and real-time problem resolution strengthened customer confidence in their brand.

Results Speak for Themselves

With these strategies, Lucas' business not only survived, but thrived. Integrating ChatGPT into his business strategy resulted in a 50% increase in customer retention and a 75% increase in sales conversions. His online store began to receive recognition not only for its products but also for innovation in customer experience.

The Way Forward

Lucas' story illustrates the versatility and potential of ChatGPT when used strategically within any business. As our protagonist prepares to embark upon his entrepreneurial journey, it becomes apparent that AI is more than a technology tool; it can bring business success.

Lucas' adventures show readers how the theory can be implemented realistically and practically, providing not only an enthralling tale but also valuable lessons on using ChatGPT in the world of e-commerce. Each chapter serves as an indispensable guide to helping navigate digital age challenges while discovering what AI offers online businesses.

As Lucas moves forward with his quest for an interdependent future between technology and humanity, readers can anticipate each new chapter to apply these lessons to their own entrepreneurial initiatives. Lucas' tale serves as an inspiration, reminding readers that within every digital interaction lies an opportunity waiting to be discovered.

CHAPTER 5

THE AI ENTREPRENEUR: TRANSFORMING CHATGPT INTO PROFIT

Lucas opened his eyes at dawn to find his mind filled with new thoughts that had percolated throughout the night. He remembered when his passion for technology had only been an interest, now blossoming into reality. What had begun as a game to connect people using ChatGPT, now defined his new reality.

Lucas began his journey through an innocent dialogue. He used ChatGPT to provide personalized recommendations to visitors and noticed something astonishing: the responses generated were not only relevant but also created with the potential to prompt action.

Each question and exchange led directly toward potential transactions with ChatGPT helping each user through each journey to purchase. Lucas unwittingly established an effective sales tool through each dialogue exchanged.

ChatGPT quickly outgrew simple interactions. Lucas used AI-powered machine learning algorithms to segment his audience, crafting ads that not only grabbed people's attention but resonated with prospective customers directly - no longer just calls to action but personalized dialogues tailored specifically for individual consumers' wants and needs - eventually turning clicks into customers who later became brand advocates!

ChatGPT's integration of affiliate platforms marked its next major advancement. Every time it suggested products, its AI generated affiliate links containing commission-generating clickable links ready for use - each click bringing with it hope of commission and proof that words could turn into actions taken.

Lucas' entry into consulting made an indelible mark. Utilizing ChatGPT to analyze data and market trends, Lucas started offering customized reports and business strategies to digital entrepreneurs using ChatGPT as their data analysis platform of choice. His expert analysis and insights established him as an authoritative voice on digital age trends while opening up a whole new revenue stream: data-driven consulting.

ChatGPT enabled him to use analytics generated by each product launch to determine not only when but also the most appropriate time and means for its release, along with any necessary promotional strategies. These launches weren't merely attempts at luck; rather, they were planned in advance with knowledge and foresight.

Lucas studied success stories similar to his own in order to adapt and implement successful strategies from them. It wasn't about imitating; rather it was a matter of understanding their core tenets and seeing if they would work on his turf. Through each adaptation and innovation he not only met market requirements but molded it to suit his vision.

Lucas was daring in his experiments on how to best monetize ChatGPT, testing everything from self-sufficient customer support systems that could close sales to AI tools for other businesses - pushing forward what was possible while expanding his empire with every new app he came up with.

Lucas not only expanded his offerings and services, but also his revenue streams. Subscriptions, exclusive products, online courses and webinars fueled the steady expansion of his digital business.

Lucas understood the value of networking networks, and Lucas used these to spread his ideas about innovation and artificial intelligence among his community of like minds. Lucas used networking networks as fertile ground to sow future collaborations - many of which turned into business opportunities.

Lucas found strength in his community not only because it provided new insights and resources, but also as a space to experiment collaboratively. Through connections made, webinars attended, and conversations had, all became sources of motivation and growth - an environment in which sharing knowledge was equally as rewarding as selling products or services he offered.

Lucas understood that success wasn't an event but rather a process to be measured against. Each new venture, product launch, and service provided was approached with meticulous analysis and experimentation; constantly seeking ways to expand and better his reach. Lucas understood that success wasn't something achieved overnight but rather through sustained hard work toward an expanded vision.

Lucas' consulting services quickly gained in popularity. Not only could he perform data analysis, but also personalization and strategy implementation services. Lucas offered more than reports; clients wanted to know how they could leverage data in their marketing campaigns, offers or conversion optimization - and Lucas knew all the answers.

One day while reviewing sales and engagement reports, an epiphany occurred: ChatGPT wasn't simply a tool; it was his business partner. Together they had turned his passion into their profession; every conversation, line of code, or piece of feedback had played an instrumental part.

Lucas recognized his story was an inspirational example of the power of AI combined with human vision and effort, so it became important for him to share his journey so others could replicate his success. So, he started writing a book detailing everything from humble beginnings through to ChatGPT's successful monetization.

The book was meticulously organized, outlining every step he had taken with ChatGPT to capitalize on his passion: from turning conversations into sales to developing tailored marketing and advertising plans; including how it integrated with affiliate platforms and predictive data analytics could become winning business strategies.

He didn't leave anything out - his book provided a comprehensive approach for turning curiosity into a lucrative career, outlining how to diversify revenue streams, use ChatGPT to form the basis of consulting work, and how networking could turn stagnant businesses into flourishing ones.

But Luke's book wasn't just an advice book; it was also an account of his transformation, with each chapter reflecting upon lessons he had learned, obstacles overcome and triumphant victories achieved along his journey.

Lucas couldn't help but feel an immense sense of gratitude towards ChatGPT, the technology that had enabled his journey. ChatGPT had more than been just another program; it had led to a profound personal transformation for himself and now with this book he hoped that similar change could spread among others.

Lucas' story had become an inspiration to those looking to enter the field of artificial intelligence; those who saw ChatGPT not as just another chatbot but as a step toward an artificially intelligent future. It served as proof that with hard work and determination turning an interest into a profession was both possible and inevitable.

Lucas had found his niche in the fast-paced world of technology and digital business, and with his book could now apply the principles and strategies that helped him monetize ChatGPT to provide valuable resources to readers.

Luke's book was met with great acclaim upon publication, not only because its content was invaluable but also as an example for living. Each sale, download, and positive review served as validation of his journey - signs that his story resonated with those looking to turn their passions into professions themselves.

Luke knew that writing his book was only the start. While its principles could help others build upon them, only their practical application could bring real change. Therefore he began offering workshops and courses, expanding on what had been learned theoretically into tangible practice.

Lucas designed each workshop session so it was interactive and accessible, ensuring even those without technical backgrounds could understand and apply its lessons.

Lucas led these sessions and taught attendees how to utilize ChatGPT to analyze their conversations for potential monetization opportunities. He demonstrated how ChatGPT responses could be leveraged to generate leads, implement affiliate links organically, and set up consulting services utilizing deep data analysis provided by AI.

Each workshop concluded with case studies from attendees, where together they explored specific examples of how monetization strategies could be adapted to their businesses. This not only enhanced learning, but also created a supportive and learning community among participants long after the workshop had come and gone.

Lucas fostered ongoing innovation by encouraging participants to experiment with ChatGPT applications. He encouraged them to consider how AI might address specific problems within their niche markets, providing the framework necessary for testing ideas risk-free.

Lucas carefully documented additional success stories as they came about through this process, enriching his teaching material while also showing AI's versatility and potential across a wide variety of industries. From entrepreneurs in e-commerce to healthcare professionals, the success stories demonstrated ChatGPT's adaptability in adapting its monetization strategies to diverse environments.

Lucas understood success not just in terms of revenue generated but also by its impact on people's lives. Watching others achieve their goals and realize their dreams was highly satisfying to him, while each new entrepreneur who found their path through his book or workshops represented another chapter in his own journey.

Lucas' book and workshops served as an inspirational starting point for many, but the true mark of his success lay in the transformational change and innovation it unleashed. Lucas' story wasn't simply one man and an AI; rather it illustrated how knowledge and technology could empower individuals in their pursuit of fulfilling and profitable careers.

Lucas' journey from experimenting with ChatGPT as a hobby to turning it into a successful business model has become an inspiration to others. His story demonstrated the vast possibilities open up by harnessing curiosity, creativity, and technology - and now his legacy would pave the way for others who sought to turn their hobbies into careers guided by Lucas' monetization strategies and unyielding spirit.

Monetization Strategies: From ChatGPT to Revenue Generation

Lucas places particular emphasis in Chapter Four on how to transition from tinkering with an idea to real revenue generation through AI. Here, he offers a pragmatic formula with key steps and concrete examples of turning ChatGPT skills into revenue streams.

Lucas skillfully avoids lengthy theoretical explanations by getting right down to business: How to turn ChatGPT conversations into cash flow. Here is his concise, action-oriented outline:

1. **Identifying Revenue Opportunities**: Here, Lucas illustrates with examples how to identify opportunities that have monetization potential. For example, he shares a story of a user who created an interactive gardening guide using ChatGPT, answering frequently asked questions and then selling the guide as a digital product.
2. **ChatGPT on Marketing and Advertising**: He shows how to train ChatGPT to develop ad copy or blog content that drives SEO and engagement. Through a case study, he reveals how

a small business increased their conversion rate by 30% with ads written by ChatGPT.

3. **Integration with Affiliate Programs**: Lucas provides a template for integrating affiliate product recommendations into ChatGPT responses, detailing how one technology blogger increased his affiliate revenue by including personalized product recommendations based on conversations users were having with the AI within his blog.
4. **ChatGPT-based consulting**: With examples from his own experience, Lucas describes how to use ChatGPT to offer consulting, such as a CV writing service where ChatGPT provides the first version and the consultant provides the final customization.
5. **Data Analysis for Product Launches**: Through a step-by-step narrative, Lucas shares how to analyze ChatGPT conversations to gain market insights and improve product launch strategies. He cites an entrepreneur who refined his product offering based on the most frequently asked questions users were asking ChatGPT.

Success Stories and Adaptation to Specific Niches

This chapter includes success stories to motivate readers. For example, it describes how one fitness content creator used ChatGPT to develop customized workouts and nutrition advice which he then offered as premium packages.

Lucas urges readers to view ChatGPT not as a universal solution but as a flexible tool that should be tailored specifically to their audience and needs. Through hands-on exercises, he guides them in fine-tuning ChatGPT's capabilities for their niche market - from initial setup through monitoring and optimizing based on user feedback.

Direct Conclusion: Monetization in Action

Lucas ends this chapter by emphasizing action. He emphasizes the need for experimentation and continuous iterative learning rather than dwelling solely on theory, encouraging readers to put his advice into action while adapting it as necessary along the way.

At the conclusion of this chapter, readers have gained not only an overview of monetization tactics; they have seen how these techniques are applied in real life situations and markets alike - they're ready to apply them as part of their journey toward monetizing ChatGPT!

CHAPTER 6

THE ART OF AI COMMUNICATION: CRAFTING PROMPTS FOR SUCCESS

As the author of this digital transformation journey, I find myself reflecting on the steps that have led Emma and Lucas to achieve their longed-for financial freedom or entrepreneurial success. It is fascinating how Artificial Intelligence and, in particular, ChatGPT have been crucial tools in their success. Their ability to master prompts has been key, turning simple interactions into valuable, revenue-generating conversations.

Let me share with you, dear reader, how I have mastered the art of formulating prompts, transforming this knowledge into a highly profitable competency.

Mastering Prompt Creation: The Secret to High Income

Prompts are the essence of how we communicate our needs and desires to AI. It's not simply asking questions or giving commands; it's a subtle art that, when perfected, unlocks incredible potential.

Designing prompts that not only connect, but also convert

Let's begin by covering the fundamentals of creating effective prompts. Clarity is of utmost importance here - an easily understood prompt can guide ChatGPT towards producing an equally clear and valuable answer, such as this example "How can I increase the click-through rate on my emails?" which tells the AI exactly what information it needs from you and is action-oriented.

A/B testing and optimizing prompts to maximize conversions is another essential element. Let's say you want to find an engaging way of encouraging subscribers to subscribe to your newsletter; using ChatGPT you could test two versions of prompts against one another and see which prompt yields more desirable responses from your users.

Personalizing content requires knowing how to tailor prompts to different audiences. For example, businesspeople would expect formal and direct language. On the other hand, youth fashion blogs would likely feature more creative responses - for instance "Give me some conservative investment strategies" could become "What fashion trends will dominate this year?" as examples of this adaptation.

Grammarly or Hemingway plugins can help streamline and automate prompt creation, helping ensure clarity and conciseness in every prompt you create.

Utilizing data and metrics to further hone and perfect your prompts is of vital importance. Examining user responses generated by your prompts can yield invaluable insight that allows you to adjust your approach accordingly.

Tips and strategies to optimize your prompts and maximize your ROI

Understanding the psychology behind effective prompts can make all the difference in user response to ChatGPT. Humans tend to enjoy the narrative, problem-solving and conflict resolution activities - all aspects which should be integrated into prompts used on ChatGPT. This will make ChatGPT's responses resonate more with users.

Calls to action are essential components of persuasion. A request such as "Give me an engaging summary of this product that concludes with an impactful question" can generate engagement quickly.

Avoiding common errors and technical difficulties is of utmost importance, since poorly worded prompts may result in irrelevant or incorrect responses that damage your credibility and undermine its foundation.

Modify prompts on an ongoing basis to take account of algorithm changes and user feedback. What works now may no longer do so in a few hours; stay adaptable.

By applying advanced copywriting techniques to your prompts, it's possible to substantially improve ChatGPT responses. Active voice, inclusion of powerful words, and creating urgency are just a few techniques you can employ in making them more impactful.

This chapter is meant to be both theoretical and practical in nature, sharing both my knowledge and experience as well as providing tangible examples that you can put into action immediately.

By the end of this chapter, my goal is that you'll feel equipped to use ChatGPT in an effective and efficient manner that enables you to reach your goals most effectively. Let's go deeper into this topic by providing examples that you can imitate.

Let's put effective prompt design into practice. Imagine you run a technology blog and need fresh article ideas for it; an effective prompt might include, "Please provide five article ideas about emerging tech that would appeal to IT professionals between 25-35."

With such an accurate prompt in place, ChatGPT can generate responses that not only pertain to the topic of interest but are likely to reach your target audience as well.

Let's say you want to test two prompts when A/B testing prompts, such as optimizing a Facebook ad: Two different ChatGPT prompts could include "Create copy for a Facebook ad that highlights the benefits of photo editing software" and "Generate eye-catching copy for a Facebook ad about photo editing software for professionals and enthusiasts". You could compare responses in terms of clicks and conversions and determine which prompt is more successful in driving clicks and conversions.

Imagine that you sell online cooking courses. A bespoke prompt might include, "Write an introduction that resonates with foodies who enjoy cooking with family." ChatGPT could then produce responses which emphasize sharing experiences while celebrating home cooking; which are more likely to appeal to your target audience.

Let's consider tools and plugins. WordPress users can take advantage of the Yoast SEO plugin to optimize prompts for SEO; Yoast can then help analyze and improve responses provided to you through prompts like: "Give me SEO headline suggestions for an article about sustainable living".

Imagine you are measuring the effectiveness of abandoned cart email prompts: your initial prompt may have been, for example, "Write an engaging email to recover customers who have abandoned their shopping cart," then measure the open rate and cart recovery rate; if results were insufficiently satisfying you might change to something like: "Compose an engaging email with a limited time offer to recover abandoned carts" before comparing results again.

As part of your marketing strategies and tricks, let's apply psychological principles behind effective prompts. Say you are creating a campaign for a fitness product; an effective prompt might include "Please share a personal transformation story that illustrates the need for positive life changes that our product facilitates". This uses psychological storytelling principles that create powerful responses with audiences.

One way of engaging readers would be through calls to action; an example might include, "Write a blog article urging readers to register for our free webinar on financial health. ChatGPT provides text which not only summarizes its contents, but also convinces them to take the desired action.

To avoid common mistakes, ensure your prompts are specific enough. Instead of asking for marketing tips in general terms like, "Give me some marketing tips", consider specifying, "Generate five low-cost marketing strategies for startups in the digital wellness industry".

If your marketing emails seem impersonal, adjust your prompt accordingly: "Write a marketing email that sounds more friendly and approachable, targeting those interested in self-care products.

Applying advanced copywriting techniques to your prompts, you could say: "Create an engaging blog title using curiosity and urgency to draw readers in and educate them on smart cryptocurrency investments.

These examples provide a glimpse of the complexity and potential of well-designed prompts. By applying these concepts in practice and adapting your prompts based on concrete results, you will fine-tune your interactions with AI so they engage your target audience while driving action and conversions.

As another way of avoiding common errors, let's say you have noticed that ChatGPT articles for your blog lack emotional resonance. Adjusting prompts may be one way of combatting this; for instance, instead of "Write an article about cyber security" asking "Write a captivating narrative about how cyber security can prevent startup disasters with testimonials and shocking statistics", providing emotional elements can strengthen relationships between reader and writer and create greater engagement between them both.

Keep Your Prompts Current AI is constantly developing new algorithms. Thus, it is vital that prompts remain current. If the effectiveness of your customer service prompts has lessened over time, reviewing recent changes to ChatGPT and adapting them may be necessary; you could switch from "Providing answers to frequently asked questions about our software" to "Providing detailed and empathetic responses that highlight new software features while offering practical examples".

Imagine you need to enhance product descriptions on your online store. A suitable prompt would be "Write product descriptions that use storytelling techniques to highlight benefits, uniqueness and urgency associated with each product" This directive requires ChatGPT to employ specific copywriting strategies that have proven their worth in increasing conversion rates.

Understanding how persuasive elements work within your prompts will give you a significant edge. For instance, using "Create a narrative that illustrates how our life coaching service can assist individuals overcome common obstacles, using success statistics and real testimonials to build credibility." This type of prompt not only solicits information but is designed to establish trust by showing value through social proof.

Final note: I encourage you to experiment with these concepts. Although the theory behind creating prompts may be complex and dense, practice will lead to mastery. Explore different styles and structures when creating prompts; pay close attention to responses received and optimize accordingly; remembering that clarity and intention are your greatest assets when communicating with artificial intelligence (AI).

Implement these detailed and practical approaches, and you will take one step closer to realizing your dream income by turning every prompt into a golden opportunity. Mastering prompt creation lies in being able to transform seemingly simple questions into golden chances for your business or venture - with each perfectly-crafted prompt you build ChatGPT into an effective digital weapon in your arsenal.

With these examples and strategies in mind, your journey to mastering prompt creation should be clear. Through practice and continuous evaluation of results, you can hone your skills and use AI not simply as content creation tool but as strategic partner on your journey. Effective prompt creation requires effective communication; conversing fluently in AI's language means more efficiently reaching business and financial goals.

One popular technique to enhance interaction with ChatGPT is "impersonate..." This approach involves asking ChatGPT to assume the persona or approach of an expert, historical figure, fictional character or even conceptual entity in order to answer questions and generate content.

Applying this technique, your prompt might look something like this: "Imagine you are an internationally recognized nutrition expert - can you explain to me why the Mediterranean diet is important?" This enables ChatGPT to contextualize responses more creatively and accurately; thus creating unique content which may resonate differently with different audiences.

ChatGPT will focus on developing content that not only informs but also exudes the professionalism and authority of an experienced financial coach.

Note that while using ChatGPT can elicit interesting and imaginative responses, its use must always be done responsibly to respect both copyrights and image of those it emulates.

Applying this technique and the strategies discussed throughout this chapter, you can transform how you engage with AI to produce content that not only attracts but also converts, establishing yourself as an authoritative figure online and efficiently monetizing your efforts.

At this stage in this chapter, it's essential to recognize that mastering ChatGPT prompts is an ongoing journey. Experimentation and continuous adaptation are keys to staying ahead of the game; through intelligent application of these methods you may unlock revenue opportunities similar to Emma and Lucas have leveraged. Ultimately AI tools such as ChatGPT offer infinite potential; all it requires is your skill at finding ways to navigate them effectively in order to maximize them.

CHAPTER 7

AUTOMATION AND SCALABILITY WITH CHATGPT - A NEW FRONTIER IN DIGITAL BUSINESS

As I ponder Emma and Lucas' journeys, it becomes evident that both found financial independence through innovation, creativity, and strategic application of cutting-edge technology. Being an author and expert at the intersection of artificial intelligence and digital entrepreneurship, I have witnessed first-hand its transformative power - in particular ChatGPT. Here I share with you my experiences and insights for using ChatGPT to automate and scale your business into an efficient and profitable enterprise.

Effective Automation to Multiply Revenue Streams

Automation at its core involves simplifying and improving processes through technology. ChatGPT takes this concept a step further by automating not only repetitive tasks but also complex communication and customer service components - opening up endless opportunities for online business.

My own experience provided a tangible example: ChatGPT was deployed on my ecommerce website to automate responses to frequently asked customer questions, not only reducing support team workload but also providing instant and accurate answers to customer inquiries - leading to both increased customer satisfaction and reduced operating costs. The impact was significant: an increase in customer satisfaction while simultaneously decreasing operating costs.

Automation with ChatGPT extends beyond customer support. As mentioned in earlier chapters, one area that benefits significantly is content marketing. My company relies on AI-generated ideas, article outlines, and even full drafts for content creation purposes; this enables a consistent stream of fresh, relevant material crucial for SEO and user engagement - without incurring man hours traditionally needed for its creation.

The Art of Scalability in Digital Business through AI

Scalability refers to expanding and adapting your business in an efficient manner, using AI for managing higher interaction volumes or expanding capabilities without increasing resources requirements. In the context of this chapter, this implies using AI to facilitate rapid expansion without incurring proportional increases in costs.

One area I have applied this to is customer data analysis. Utilizing ChatGPT to examine large sets of customer behavior data allows me to gain valuable insights about their preferences and behaviors that can inform strategic decisions for product development, marketing personalization and improving the customer experience.

Another key use for ChatGPT is creating customized product recommendation systems. By analyzing customers' past interactions and purchasing habits, ChatGPT can generate highly tailored recommendations that improve not only shopping experiences but also conversion rates and average order values.

Let's consider an example to demonstrate the applicability of ChatGPT concepts to business. Say you run a wellness and lifestyle blog: ChatGPT can automatically generate personalized responses to reader comments, increasing community and increasing engagement while at the same time providing ideas for articles or series based on trends detected from user interactions.

Scalability manifests itself here by maintaining high levels of engagement and fresh content with relatively less effort, freeing you to focus on other areas of your business. Artificial Intelligence allows you to clone yourself, multiplying yourself without increasing staff proportionally as your company expands.

Automation and scalability are at the core of a successful digital business, offering us an exceptional opportunity to redefine these concepts within our companies. Implementing ChatGPT strategically not only increases efficiency and costs while simultaneously increasing customer satisfaction and opening new revenue streams.

Continued exploration of ChatGPT has led me to discover its powerful impact and to examine its practical applications and strategic benefits more thoroughly.

My goal is to equip you with both theoretical knowledge and practical guidelines/examples you can immediately implement into your business or offer as services to other organizations.

Practical and In-Depth ChatGPT Applications

The possibilities of AI are endless, but I'd like to show you where companies are already integrating ChatGPT and it is generating workload savings while creating more scalable businesses.

1. **The Customer Service Revolution**: As previously described, ChatGPT can be utilized as part of a system that handles basic customer queries while your support team focuses on more complex cases. Many companies are actively looking for such solutions and digital businesses especially likely experience high numbers of queries that require equipment and staff for them to handle them effectively. AI technology has made customer support simpler than ever, which we will see more of using ChatGPT within this field over time.

Customer service can be one of the most costly aspects of running any business, yet ChatGPT provides an elegant solution, automating initial customer interactions. I implemented ChatGPT into my business to handle common inquiries, which allowed my team to focus on more complex inquiries or high value tasks.

One application of ChatGPT integration into our online chat system was providing instantaneous answers to customer inquiries, improving both their experience and helping reduce support team workload. This led to greater customer satisfaction as well as shorter response times resulting in decreased response times for support tickets.

2. **Scalable Content Generation**: No more waiting around for inspiration; thousands of content creators worldwide use ChatGPT to generate ideas, appealing titles and draft articles for their blog or website - providing an uninterrupted supply of fresh and engaging material necessary for SEO and user engagement.

Many readers would agree with me when I say content reigns supreme in the digital realm, yet its production can be resource

intensive. ChatGPT revolutionizes this process by providing you with an efficient means to scale content production without compromising quality - in my case using it to develop blog outlines, social media updates and video scripts which helped maintain an engaging online presence essential to building and growing an audience.

As an illustration of how useful ChatGPT could be, I leveraged it when developing publications about emerging trends in technology. By providing ChatGPT with my list of key topics and quickly receiving detailed outlines for each post that could then be edited by my team and refined as necessary, this strategy not only expedited content creation but also ensured it remained informative, timely and pertinent for my target audience.

3. **Marketing Automation**: Manage online advertising tools like Facebook Ads and Amazon Ads is often an ongoing task of budget adjustments and maintenance. Thanks to ChatGPT, aspects of marketing can now be automated with artificial intelligence making decisions on its own about when or if more funds should be invested or optimized CPC (Cost Per Click) metrics or other measures should be prioritized.

Personalization is a cornerstone of advertising campaigns in general, and ChatGPT makes this task effortless yet remarkably effective. In my own experience with email campaigns using this approach, open and click-through rates increased substantially thanks to targeted prompts generated by ChatGPT that resonated more with specific segments based on their interests and past behaviors.

Example: when targeting customers interested in fitness products, prompts were designed to focus on health and exercise-related topics;

in contrast, emails sent to nutrition-minded customers included healthy recipes and diet tips.

4. **Predictive Analytics for Decision Making**: ChatGPT companies have found an efficient system to feed it with continuous inputs and produce near real-time analytics that allow for fast decision-making. ChatGPT can be used to analyze customer and market data and predict trends; adjust buying patterns; manage inventory strategies; or even assist with strategic business planning decisions.

Data is an invaluable source of insights and opportunities in today's globalized world, and ChatGPT makes automating data analysis much simpler for you to unlock it all. I used ChatGPT extensively when analyzing customer behavior patterns and market trends - it helped adjust my marketing strategy accordingly and identify new product opportunities.

Analyzing customer interaction data using ChatGPT enabled me to quickly identify the most requested products and most frequent searches on my website, providing critical insights that enabled me to adjust inventory levels and enhance product descriptions both on the marketplaces I sold on as well as my ecommerce storefront. Integrating ChatGPT into your digital business could prove transformative not only in how it operates but also how your customers perceive you and increase sales in an ever more competitive marketplace.

Concrete Tools for ChatGPT Integration

One key to making the most of ChatGPT is using the right tools for its integration and systematization in your business. Let me share

some tools I have found effective from my own experience that could work in yours too.

1. **Zapier for Workflow Automation**: Zapier is an automation tool that lets you automate workflows across various applications by linking them together. For instance, Zapier makes it possible to integrate ChatGPT with CRMs such as Salesforce to automate data entry of customer interactions into each of them - keeping an efficient and quality customer follow up system in place.
2. **Hootsuite for Social Media Management**: Hootsuite is a social media management tool that can be combined with ChatGPT to schedule and publish content. You can use ChatGPT to generate draft posts and then use Hootsuite to schedule them, ensuring a constant and consistent presence on your social media platforms.
3. **Google Analytics for Data Analysis**: Google Analytics is an invaluable asset to any digital business, and by integrating it with ChatGPT you can analyze user behavior on your website to generate personalized prompts that improve user experience and drive conversions.
4. **MailChimp for Email Marketing Campaigns**: MailChimp is an email marketing platform that can be combined with ChatGPT to develop and send targeted email campaigns. ChatGPT can generate the content for these emails before using MailChimp to segment users based on their interests and behaviors, sending personalized emails based on personalized settings within MailChimp.

Conclusion: A Future Driven by ChatGPT

As we near the conclusion of this chapter, my aim is to summarize what has been learned thus far and provide an outlook for the future with ChatGPT as a key tool in transforming your business. My objective has been to give a practical yet in-depth understanding of how ChatGPT can not only enhance efficiency in operations but also help scale your company successfully and sustainably.

ChatGPT: More than Automation, a Business Revolution

ChatGPT isn't simply an automation tool; it represents a fundamental shift in our digital business approach. Thanks to its capabilities for handling everything from customer service and content production to data analytics, this digital business platform affords entrepreneurs like yourself and me an unprecedented chance to reinvent how we run and scale our businesses.

Integrating ChatGPT into your business goes far beyond automating processes or cutting workload. Instead, it transforms how you connect with customers, enhance their experiences, and offer services and products that not only meet their needs but anticipate and surpass expectations.

AI will become ever more vital to running efficient, responsive, and customer-centric businesses of tomorrow. By adopting this technology for yourself or your organization, not only can you remain ahead in an increasingly competitive marketplace but you will be offering unique customer experiences to set it apart from rival businesses.

Smart and strategic use of ChatGPT can catapult your business to new heights of success. From automating customer service, customizing marketing efforts, analyzing large amounts of data for insights to automating customer support; all are just some examples of its many uses in modern businesses. It all boils down to how this tool fits into your overall business strategy.

For optimal implementation of ChatGPT within your business, customization and continuous adaptation must be prioritized. ChatGPT should not be applied as a one-size-fits-all solution but instead used to meet specific business and customer needs effectively.

Never underestimate the impact of ChatGPT on your business. Use tools and metrics to evaluate its efficacy, then adjust as necessary. By regularly monitoring and adapting this powerful tool, you'll maximize its benefits.

At this chapter's conclusion, I urge each reader to commit themselves to an innovative path of growth and transformation. ChatGPT should not simply be seen as another tool; rather it represents an investment into your company's future - its capacity for automation, customization and scaling is immense; by learning to effectively utilize ChatGPT you are giving yourself and your company the best chance for future success and happiness.

Always ensure that you measure and evaluate the impact of ChatGPT on your business, using tools and metrics to assess its efficacy and make changes as needed. By constantly monitoring and adapting, ChatGPT's full benefits will be realized.

Artificial Intelligence can play a pivotal role in increasing efficiency and customer focus for businesses of all kinds, so I encourage you to embrace AI as your partner in building an efficient, scalable customer-focused organization. ChatGPT can unlock untold potential within your business and propel it to new levels of success - so start taking advantage of AI automation today and begin creating it now!

CHAPTER 8

CREATING STRATEGIC ALLIANCES IN THE AI ECOSYSTEM

On my journey through Artificial Intelligence, I have come to appreciate that one key to unlocking its full potential with tools such as ChatGPT is building strategic partnerships. As we delve further into AI ecosystem, new opportunities arise for collaboration; business world experts and references arise thanks to this revolution; we will discuss ways of building networks and lucrative collaborations, as well as investigating technology integration possibilities in this chapter.

Networks and Lucrative Collaborations with Other Professionals and Technologies

First and foremost, establishing strong networks is crucial. In the ever-evolving digital environment, collaboration with professionals and technologies is absolutely key for success. AI cannot stand on its own; rather it exists within an ecosystem of entrepreneurs and developers where synergies can help us achieve greater results faster than alone.

Effective networking begins by finding professionals who share your goals and vision. For example, imagine you are an expert in digital marketing services; if you don't keep up-to-date on current trends and advances, competitors could begin offering more attractive products or services, or growing more efficiently thanks to artificial intelligence (AI).

But this situation could work both ways; if AI is clearly the solution to your competition issues, keeping abreast of developments and how they apply to your industry can give you a competitive advantage and beat them at their game. Join communities discussing AI/ChatGPT news/events/debates; attend key conferences/events/debate discussions as a reference; participate in debates/discussions at major conferences/events etc. - your competitors will see you as an authority figure and can only watch how you expand their businesses as time passes by!

Online forums and AI communities provide an ideal space to network with like-minded people who share similar goals. You can use ChatGPT to address specific inquiries that arise within these communities or generate content that you can share, establishing yourself as an active member and subject matter expert.

Once connections have been formed, the next step should be undertaking collaborative projects. For instance, if you know someone with expertise in data analytics, perhaps working together on creating a service or product that combines ChatGPT skills with their data expertise to offer customers something more complete and attractive than what was available before.

Search for technological integrations

Integration of technologies is also of vital importance: ChatGPT alone is powerful; when combined with other technologies, its potential increases exponentially.

An effective approach is integrating AI tools. For instance, ChatGPT could be used alongside sentiment analysis tools that use its reach to not only generate content but also gauge its emotional resonance with audiences. Where its basic version cannot reach, plugins and integrations may fill any gaps.

ChatGPT's success during the second half of 2023 made it clear that technology integration will become not only a strategy, but an absolute requirement in the artificial intelligence landscape of tomorrow. In this chapter, we will explore how partnerships and integrations can open doors to new business opportunities - strategies which you too can employ on your journey towards financial freedom.

Offering Integral Solutions

Customers today appreciate solutions that meet multiple needs simultaneously. If you offer marketing services, ChatGPT could help generate content, analytics tools could evaluate performance, and automation tools would then distribute this across various platforms - prompts might include "Develop a comprehensive content strategy for a sustainable fashion brand, including keyword analysis and recommendations for content distribution automation.

Technology integration can also significantly enhance user experiences. If you manage an e-learning platform, ChatGPT could offer personalized tutorials and interactive support; an effective prompt may include "Create a virtual assistant to provide personalized explanations and practical examples for Python programming courses.

Combining ChatGPT with AI technologies can transform customer support systems. Imagine an AI system where ChatGPT not only answers questions, but can also anticipate and offer solutions for future issues based on user behavioral data analysis. An example prompt for such use might be: "Generate proactive responses to technical support queries while anticipating common problems and providing preventive solutions".

Creating Dynamic Content

Marketing and advertising professionals know the power of dynamic and personalized content creation is immense. By using ChatGPT with data analytics tools, marketers and advertisers can generate dynamic ads that respond immediately to user preferences and behaviors in real-time based on demographic and interaction data. A great prompt for this might be: "Create personalized social media ads targeted to different audience segments using demographic and interaction data".

Collaboration between experts in different fields can open up opportunities you never thought existed. While ChatGPT alone can be effective, pairing experts in certain sectors or fields with AI makes an unstoppable combination.

ChatGPT could become an appealing technology product by working alongside psychologists to develop self-help and mindfulness tools, creating self-help solutions many would desire. A prompt might read, "Create an AI-based mindfulness program that adapts to user emotional needs using daily feedback from information provided. Each day we will collect new learnings gathered through patients for your AI to access. With enough data collected by ChatGPT's AI system, ChatGPT could produce tools or software which assist users while offering psychologists another value-add service they could add.

Integrating ChatGPT with automation tools is an invaluable asset when scaling your business. As we've explored throughout this book, AI integrations with tools businesses already use will become increasingly prevalent - from automating frequently asked questions (FAQs), offering inventory management solutions and processing orders more efficiently, through to offering easy to interpret Google Analytics reports - opening up endless possibilities that make every day work simpler for everyone involved.

Using CRM for Customer Personalization

Customer relationship management (CRM) tools such as Salesforce or HubSpot can be integrated with ChatGPT to create highly personalized customer experiences. You can configure ChatGPT to generate automated communications based on customer information stored in your CRM. An example prompt would be: "Create a personalized follow-up email for customers who have purchased products in the technology category in the last 30 days, offering them complementary products."

Custom Chatbots Development with Dialog flow

Google's Dialog flow is a tool for creating conversational interfaces such as chatbots. By integrating ChatGPT with Dialog flow, you can develop more sophisticated and customized chatbots for your website or application. For example, you could create a chatbot that uses ChatGPT to answer technical questions from your customers about your products in a more natural and detailed way.

Improving Customer Experience with Intercom

Intercom is an enterprise messaging platform that enables communication with customers. By integrating ChatGPT with

Intercom, you can automate responses to common questions and provide immediate assistance, enhancing the customer experience. You could configure ChatGPT to provide instant responses to frequently asked questions, while collecting data for future, more personalized interactions.

Content Optimization with SEMrush

SEMrush is a digital marketing tool that provides SEO, PPC, content and social media data. By integrating ChatGPT with SEMrush, you can optimize your content for search engines and social media. A useful prompt would be, "Use SEMrush data to generate content ideas that align with the most popular keywords in my niche market."

Predictive Analytics with IBM Watson

IBM Watson offers a range of AI services, including predictive analytics. By integrating ChatGPT with IBM Watson, you can perform more complex analytics, such as predicting market trends or customer behaviors. A suitable prompt might be, "Combine ChatGPT capabilities with IBM Watson to predict upcoming trends in the fashion market for next year."

Integration with Design Tools such as Canva

Canva is a graphic design tool that facilitates the creation of visual content. By integrating ChatGPT with Canva, you can automate the creation of visual content that complements your generated texts. For example, you could use ChatGPT to generate design descriptions and then use Canva to create visuals that align with those descriptions. A prompt might be, "Describe ideas for infographics that illustrate trends in renewable energy use," and then use these ideas as the basis for your designs in Canva.

Use of Project Management Tools such as Trello or Asana.

Integrating ChatGPT with project management tools like Trello or Asana can improve team coordination and task management. Imagine using ChatGPT to automatically generate and assign tasks based on team discussions or project updates. An example prompt would be, "Based on the last team meeting, list the outstanding tasks and assign each to the corresponding team members in Asana."

E-commerce innovation with Shopify

If you operate an online store using Shopify, integrating ChatGPT can improve user experience and operational efficiency. You could use ChatGPT to generate product descriptions, answer customer questions, or even to assist in the checkout process. A useful prompt would be, "Generate detailed and engaging descriptions for new products in our Shopify store, focusing on their unique features and benefits."

Continuous Improvement with Feedback and Analysis

In addition to technology integration, it is essential to collect and analyze feedback to continuously improve your strategies and tools. ChatGPT can help you analyze customer comments and suggestions, generating valuable insights for continuous improvement. For example, you could use a prompt such as: "Analyze recent reviews of our products and suggest areas for improvement based on customer feedback".

Conclusion and Future Perspective

As you come to the end of this chapter, my hope is that you feel inspired and equipped with all of the tools and strategies necessary to form strategic partnerships and take full advantage of technology integration into AI ecosystem. From data analytics platforms integration through user experience enhancement and product innovation. there are so many possibilities!

Success and monetization in the digital realm require creativity, adaptability and an ever-evolved mindset. By forging strategic partnerships and exploring technology integration opportunities, you will not only expand your capabilities and reach but also remain at the forefront of digital innovation.

Success in artificial intelligence and digital technology requires constant experimentation and adaptation. By keeping an open and proactive attitude, you will be better suited to take advantage of emerging opportunities while meeting challenges posed by this ever-evolving field.

In this chapter, we will focus on ethically and securely navigating monetization with ChatGPT to achieve financial success while upholding accountability and transparency.

CHAPTER 9

ZERO TO HERO WITH CHATGPT: HOW COMPLETE BEGINNERS ARE BUILDING WEALTH

AI's transformative power, particularly through tools like ChatGPT, has opened up unparalleled opportunities in terms of business and service monetization. By spending significant time exploring AI-related sales, marketing, content production and creation projects like ChatGPT I have discovered an arsenal of techniques for using this platform effectively and am now sharing them here with you as detailed models that will turn your skills into profitable ventures.

1. Mastering a Skill with AI: Sales, Marketing, and Content Creation

ChatGPT is an invaluable digital marketing assistant. Not just a tool; ChatGPT serves as a powerful ally in creating captivating sales copy, writing powerful ad scripts and developing targeted strategies. Capable of processing vast amounts of customer data to understand customer trends and preferences for targeted and highly personalized campaigns - ChatGPT makes your digital marketing efforts work smarter & harder than ever.

Consider Sarah, a digital marketer. Utilizing ChatGPT, she was able to analyze customer feedback and market trends to fine-tune her marketing messages, leading to an impressive 30% increase in conversion rates - this case study serves as evidence that human creativity combined with AI precision can have powerful results.

Sarah's digital marketing career took an extraordinary leap when she adopted ChatGPT. Sarah used specific ChatGPT prompts to achieve her goals:

Analyzing Customer Feedback:

- Sarah began by asking ChatGPT to analyze customer feedback across various platforms. Her prompts included, "Analyze customer feedback from the past quarter's surveys, emails and social media comments", followed by "Identify common themes and sentiments within customer comments while summarizing key customer preferences and issues"

Market Trend Analysis:

- To stay ahead in her niche, she utilized ChatGPT to gather and analyze market data. She prompted, "Gather recent data on market trends, competitor activities, and industry forecasts in the eco-friendly product niche," and then asked for actionable insights with, "Synthesize this market data and provide insights on emerging trends and potential marketing opportunities."

Developing Targeted Marketing Strategies:

- Sarah used ChatGPT to develop detailed customer personas based on collected data, as well as come up with marketing content ideas tailored specifically for an eco-friendly customer persona. Her request: "Please create detailed customer personas."

Sales Copy Creation:

- For compelling product descriptions and email campaigns, Sarah's prompts included, "Create product descriptions for our new line of eco-friendly products," and, "Draft personalized email templates for different segments of our email list."

Performance Analysis and Optimization:

- Finally, to measure and improve her campaigns, she used prompts like, "Analyze the performance data of our recent marketing campaigns," followed by, "Suggest adjustments to optimize our current marketing strategies."

Sarah used targeted prompts from ChatGPT to maximize her digital marketing efforts, not simply automating but instead incorporating AI into creative and strategic processes - leading to significant improvements in efficiency, customer engagement and business growth for her campaigns. Sarah's story serves as proof that AI - especially ChatGPT - can transform digital marketing for those without extensive technical background.

2. Delegating Work to ChatGPT for Enhanced Productivity

ChatGPT can make all the difference when it comes to delegating mundane tasks to it, for instance social media managers who wish to automate regular updates and responses, freeing up time for more strategic tasks - leading to increased productivity and improved communication quality.

Mike, an entrepreneur, discovered the potential of ChatGPT to streamline his business operations. Feeling overwhelmed by day-to-day tasks, Mike turned to ChatGPT as a solution and was soon freed of routine tasks by delegating them to ChatGPT - freeing him to focus on strategic aspects of his business such as client consultations and team meetings. Furthermore, Mike used prompts such as, "Draft a daily schedule for managing client consultations and team meetings." Additionally for customer service inquiries Mike created prompts like, "Respond to frequently asked customer questions regarding product features or pricing." This automation not only improved response times but also ensured consistency in customer communication between teams.

Mike utilized ChatGPT beyond administrative tasks for content production and market research purposes, using prompts such as, "Create engaging blog post ideas for a tech startup" and "Examine emerging trends in the tech industry". These actions greatly increased his business's productivity by allocating resources more effectively while focusing on growth and development goals. His experience shows how small businesses can use AI tools such as ChatGPT to optimize operations and enhance overall efficiency.

3. The Agency Model: Scaling with AI

ChatGPT can play a pivotal role in agency business models that rely on AI-enhanced services, including AI-driven content creation, data analysis and chatbot development. Agencies need to attract clients who appreciate AI solutions while managing ChatGPT effectively for various tasks.

Emma, an entrepreneurial individual, employed ChatGPT's powerful AI capabilities to launch a successful marketing agency. By integrating AI into her operations, Emma was able to provide superior and efficient services for her clients - here is how ChatGPT helped Emma during various stages of agency expansion:

Agency's Initial Setup and Service Design:

- For setting up her agency, Emma used prompts like, "Generate a business plan outline for a digital marketing agency," and, "Suggest a range of digital marketing services suitable for small to medium-sized businesses."

Crafting Unique Marketing Strategies:

- Emma relied on ChatGPT to develop innovative marketing strategies. She input prompts such as, "Create a digital marketing strategy for a local bakery focusing on social media engagement," allowing her to offer tailored solutions to her clients.

Generating Creative Content:

- To provide content creation services, Emma used ChatGPT for ideas and initial drafts. Prompts like, "Draft an engaging social media campaign concept for an eco-friendly brand," helped her team in ideation and execution.

Client Communication and Relationship Management:

- Maintaining effective communication with clients was key. Emma used prompts such as, "Draft an email updating a client on their campaign progress," ensuring transparency and building trust.

Team Collaboration and Project Management:

- To manage her growing team, Emma utilized ChatGPT for internal communication and project tracking. She used prompts like, "Create a weekly task list for the content team focusing on upcoming campaign deliverables."

Scaling the Agency:

- As her agency expanded, Emma explored new verticals. She used prompts such as, "Identify potential growth areas for a digital marketing agency in the current market," allowing her to make informed decisions on scaling her business.

Training and Knowledge Sharing:

- For training new team members, Emma utilized ChatGPT to create training materials and resources. Prompts like, "Develop a training module for new hires on SEO best practices," were instrumental in upskilling her team.

Emma's journey showcases how strategically leveraging ChatGPT can significantly enhance the operations of a marketing agency. From the initial setup, crafting tailored marketing strategies, to scaling the agency and training staff, ChatGPT acted as a versatile tool that supported her in delivering high-quality services and managing her business more efficiently. Her agency's success became a testament to the innovative integration of AI in the realm of digital marketing.

4. Leveraging Platforms like Fiverr with ChatGPT

Online platforms such as Fiverr provide an excellent way of capitalizing on AI-enhanced skills. Here, you can offer AI-driven market analysis services, chatbot development or customized content creation - the key being effectively communicating the value that ChatGPT brings to these services.

John, a freelancer on Fiverr offering AI-powered content writing services, leverages ChatGPT to rapidly deliver top-quality writing at an unprecedented speed, drawing in clients of various kinds.

John quickly recognized the potential in combining his skills and ChatGPT capabilities to offer services on Fiverr. His focus included content creation, SEO optimization and customer solutions tailored specifically for him. To do this effectively on Fiverr platform he used specific ChatGPT prompts as tools.

Profile and Gig Creation:

- John began by crafting a compelling Fiverr profile and gig descriptions. He used prompts like, "Create an engaging profile bio for a digital marketing freelancer on Fiverr," and, "Draft a description for a gig offering SEO-optimized blog content creation."

SEO-Optimized Content Services:

- To offer content writing services, John prompted ChatGPT with, "Generate SEO-optimized blog post titles for the health and wellness niche," followed by, "Write a 500-word SEO-optimized article on the benefits of meditation."

Customized Client Proposals:

- For sending proposals to potential clients, John used ChatGPT for personalized and persuasive pitches. He entered prompts such as, "Draft a proposal for a potential client looking for a complete website content overhaul, emphasizing my expertise and past work."

Client Communication and Feedback:

- To maintain excellent client communication, he utilized prompts like, "Draft a message responding to a client's query about additional content marketing services," and,

"Formulate a polite request for client feedback after successful gig completion."

Expanding Services with ChatGPT Assistance:

- As he gained more confidence, John expanded his offerings on Fiverr. He used ChatGPT to brainstorm new service ideas with prompts like, "Suggest innovative digital marketing services that can be offered on Fiverr targeting small businesses."

Market Research and Strategy Development:

- To stay competitive, John used ChatGPT for market research. He prompted, "Analyze the top-performing digital marketing gigs on Fiverr and provide a strategy to differentiate my services."

Through these strategic prompts, John was able to establish a strong presence on Fiverr. He efficiently managed client work, responded promptly to inquiries, and continuously improved his services based on market trends and feedback. This approach allowed him to grow his client base and increase his earnings, showcasing the power of integrating AI tools like ChatGPT into freelance work, especially on platforms like Fiverr. John's story demonstrates how leveraging AI can create new opportunities and streamline workflows for freelancers in various fields.

5. Building and Scaling an AI-Powered Agency

ChatGPT can assist in the journey from freelancing to running an agency, making this transition smoother than ever. By automating various tasks related to growing service offerings without an increase in workload or costs.

Consider Linda, who successfully transitioned from freelance graphic designer to full-service design agency owner using ChatGPT as client communication and basic design tasks while focusing her energies on client acquisition and expansion of her business.

Linda embarked on her entrepreneurial journey by leveraging ChatGPT for her marketing agency. At first, she utilized ChatGPT primarily to generate content ideas and draft client proposals using prompts like: "Generate marketing campaign ideas for a health and wellness brand". Over time, Linda found herself using ChatGPT for more complex assignments like market analysis and strategy development using prompts such as: "Analyze digital marketing trends for fashion retailers". This approach allowed Linda to efficiently meet a range of client requirements efficiently with precision and creativity.

Linda's business experienced a dramatic transformation when she introduced specialized ChatGPT-based services. By tailoring AI solutions specifically tailored to client needs, her agency could automate various business functions for clients ranging from customer service to data analysis - this not only established her agency as a pioneer of AI-powered digital services but also significantly boosted Linda's ability to scale operations. Linda's story highlights the transformative power of AI applications on business growth; innovative AI applications revolutionizing service offerings and business operations alike.

6. The Art of Upscaling Skills Using ChatGPT

Upskilling in AI technology is vital, and ChatGPT can assist in speeding up learning in fields like digital advertising, SEO optimization and content marketing. AI provides insights, tutorials and case studies that make the learning process more efficient and effective.

Alex, an emerging SEO specialist, quickly recognized ChatGPT's potential in keeping up with SEO trends and tactics. By asking prompts such as "updating me on recent e-commerce SEO trends" or "Advanced SEO tactics for tech blogs", he was able to access cutting edge strategies which enabled him to provide innovative solutions to his clients - setting him apart from competitors.

Alex experienced great success when he turned to ChatGPT to analyze SEO data and create insightful reports, with prompts such as, "Analyze the SEO performance of this website and provide optimization recommendations." Not only did this save him considerable time but it also increased both accuracy and depth in his analyses. Alex is proof of how AI tools such as ChatGPT can elevate specialist offerings while remaining current with rapidly-evolving fields like SEO.

7. The Power of ChatGPT in Data Analysis and Strategy Formulation

ChatGPT's ability to analyze large datasets can be tremendously useful when strategizing for marketing or business development strategies. Analysis provides more informed decision making, driving growth and profitability.

Emily excelled as a business consultant by using ChatGPT to conduct thorough market and consumer behavior research. By using specific prompts such as "Analyze current market trends in the health and wellness industry" and "Identify consumer behavior shifts during COVID-19 pandemic," Emily could garner insights critical for her research.

Emily's keen understanding of market dynamics enabled her to create highly tailored strategies for her clients. For instance, she used ChatGPT to simulate various business scenarios and ask: "Predict the impact of a subscription-based model for a fitness app in the current market." The predictions and analyses provided by ChatGPT proved essential in helping clients switch over to more effective and profitable business models - further cementing her reputation as a forward-thinking and successful consultant.

8. ChatGPT in Automating and Optimizing Client Interactions

ChatGPT can play an invaluable role in customer engagement and service delivery. Through automating responses and interactions, businesses can maintain high customer engagement without needing extensive manpower - this automation includes email marketing, social media engagements and customer support activities.

Robert, who manages an online retail store, implemented ChatGPT into his operations to enhance customer service. When faced with the overwhelming number of customer inquiries and feedback he turned to AI as a solution; programming ChatGPT with prompts such as: "Provide detailed answers for common product feature inquiries" and "Generate empathic and helpful feedback responses".

Robert found this strategy revolutionized his customer interactions. Not only did it drastically reduce response times and enhance interactions, but the AI's deep knowledge of his product line and customer service policies enabled quick, helpful, accurate responses from ChatGPT that resulted in increased customer satisfaction rates as customers valued its prompt and informative replies resulting in greater loyalty and repeat business for his retail operations. ChatGPT proved its worth in improving customer relationships and fueling business success!

9. Tailoring ChatGPT for Specialized Niche Markets

ChatGPT stands out as an invaluable asset thanks to its versatility in adapting to niche markets. By customizing its responses and knowledge base, this AI can become an indispensable asset in healthcare, legal services, real estate transactions and niche hobbies alike.

Laura, an innovative fitness industry entrepreneur, recognized ChatGPT's potential to provide clients with something truly exceptional. She customized ChatGPT with specific prompts such as "Create personalized fitness plans based on individual body types and goals" and "Generate nutrition advice tailored specifically for individual dietary restrictions and preferences".

Laura used ChatGPT as a strategic move to set her business apart in an already competitive market. ChatGPT's ability to process and analyze vast amounts of fitness and nutrition data provided clients with highly personalized advice - an approach which resonated well with customers seeking something beyond generic fitness regimens or diet plans; AI-powered personalized recommendations provided immense value, like having their own personal trainer or nutritionist available at their fingertips.

Laura saw immediate and dramatic results of using ChatGPT with her business, drawing in customers attracted by customized fitness and nutrition strategies. ChatGPT not only enhanced Laura's service offering but also established it as an innovative leader in using AI for health and wellness solutions. Eventually, Laura created an enduring customer base by customizing technology to suit individual client needs - an impressive feat which proves how AI, when implemented carefully, can create valuable propositions while driving business expansion. Laura is an example of how thoughtfully implemented AI solutions can create unique value propositions which drive business expansion.

10. Using ChatGPT for Efficient Project Management

project management is at the core of any successful business. ChatGPT can assist in organizing tasks, setting reminders and managing team communications to streamline workflows and boost overall efficiency of projects.

David was well aware of the challenges involved with managing multiple projects simultaneously. The task of keeping track of tasks, deadlines and team communications proved extremely daunting; thus he turned to ChatGPT for assistance by integrating it into his project management workflow.

He used ChatGPT to set prompts such as, "Organize and update project timelines weekly" and "Coordinate team communication and task allocation efficiently." This integration revolutionized his project management. ChatGPT's ability to process and keep track of multiple project details was exceptional - updating timelines quickly, sending reminders to team members quickly, suggesting adjustments for ongoing projects quickly, etc. It proved invaluable!

AI's contribution was instrumental in streamlining communication within our team. Acting as a central hub, team members could access updates and clarifications on their tasks from here; this helped eliminate miscommunication while strengthening overall team coordination.

Under David's supervision, projects began being delivered on time and within budget to increase client satisfaction. ChatGPT enabled David to take on more projects without compromising on quality; his foresight in using AI project management not only increased team productivity but also set new standards within his organization for project delivery.

David's experience demonstrates how AI, when implemented strategically, can transform project management. By harnessing its potential to turn chaos into cohesive success.

11. ChatGPT in Enhancing Creative Processes

Creativity is essential in many businesses, particularly fields like advertising, design and content production. ChatGPT can serve as an invaluable brainstorming tool, providing new ideas, perspectives and helping to overcome creative blocks.

Sophia, an accomplished content creator, found ChatGPT an effective tool in her creative process for developing engaging new material. Her main objective was to keep her writing diverse, fresh, and appealing to keep growing her audience. Here is how Sophia utilized ChatGPT:

Idea Generation for Diverse Content:

Sophia began by seeking ChatGPT's assistance in generating a range of content ideas. She used prompts like, "Generate a list of unique content ideas related to [specific theme or trend]," followed by, "Suggest various content formats for these ideas, including blog posts, videos, and social media posts."

Theme Exploration for Fresh Perspectives:

To ensure her content remained fresh, she asked ChatGPT to explore and suggest new themes. Her prompts included, "Explore upcoming trends in [her content niche] and suggest themes for future content," and, "Identify underrepresented topics in [niche] that could engage my audience."

Audience Engagement Strategies:

Understanding her audience's preferences was crucial. Sophia prompted, "Analyze the engagement data of my past content," followed by, "Based on this data, suggest topics and formats that are likely to increase audience interaction and engagement."

Collaborative Content Ideas:

Sophia also explored collaborative content creation. She used prompts like, "Suggest ideas for collaborative content with other creators in [niche]," and, "Propose themes for joint projects that could appeal to both our audiences."

Content Series Development:

As part of her strategy to engage her audience more frequently, she devised content series. For each piece of the series, her prompts included, "Develop an outline based on [a particular theme or trend], as well as suggesting engaging titles and hooks for each part.

By taking advantage of tailored ChatGPT prompts, Sophia was able to successfully innovate in her content creation process. ChatGPT provided not only ideas but also insights into audience preferences and emerging trends - helping Sophia maintain a diverse content portfolio that increased engagement and helped expand her channel.

Sophia's experience with ChatGPT highlights the power of artificial intelligence (AI) to enhance creative processes and illustrates how content creators - even those without technical backgrounds - can leverage AI tools like ChatGPT in order to stay ahead in an ever-evolving digital content market.

12. Monetizing ChatGPT through Training and Workshops

Expertise in artificial intelligence tools such as ChatGPT is in high demand, making a training session or online course on its effective use an appealing business opportunity.

Mark, an expert in artificial intelligence, recognized a growing demand for AI knowledge and insight, particularly as related to ChatGPT for business growth. Recognizing this opportunity, he ventured into offering online courses and workshops through ChatGPT for business growth - this proved highly lucrative venture! Here's how he used ChatGPT effectively to design and promote his educational content:

Course Content Development:

Mark began by formulating course outlines that were informative yet accessible to a broad audience. He used prompts like, "Develop a comprehensive course outline on leveraging ChatGPT for business growth," followed by, "Break down complex AI concepts into simple, understandable modules for beginners."

Workshop Planning and Structure:

For his workshops, Mark sought to create interactive and practical sessions. He prompted ChatGPT with, "Plan a workshop itinerary that includes hands-on activities with ChatGPT for entrepreneurs," and, "Suggest engaging workshop activities that demonstrate real-world applications of ChatGPT in business."

Marketing and Promotion Strategies:

To attract attendees, Mark focused on robust marketing strategies. He used prompts such as, "Create marketing copy for social media advertising my ChatGPT courses," and, "Generate email campaign content targeting business professionals interested in AI."

Feedback Analysis for Improvement:

Post-course, Mark aimed to refine his offerings continually. He prompted, "Analyze participant feedback from the recent ChatGPT workshop," followed by, "Provide suggestions for course improvement based on the feedback."

Expansion Ideas for Future Courses:

Mark was looking to expand his course catalog, so he asked ChatGPT for innovative ideas on AI and ChatGPT topics for returning students, such as suggesting advanced course topics on these subjects or identifying emerging AI trends that can be developed into new courses.

Mark was able to use ChatGPT strategically and create and market online courses and workshops successfully using its tools, not simply capitalizing on his expertise but understanding market needs and adapting his content dynamically in response. This resulted in highly sought-after educational programs which became significant revenue generators.

Mark's journey demonstrates the potential of using AI tools like ChatGPT with domain expertise to launch new educational ventures. His journey also showcases how this combination can unlock lucrative opportunities in digital education.

13. Developing AI-Powered Products and Services

Technically inclined individuals can leverage ChatGPT's AI capabilities to their advantage by developing AI-powered products or services using it, leading to innovative yet marketable solutions like AI apps or even customized chatbot services.

Anna, an innovative software developer, quickly understood the difficulties small businesses faced in efficiently managing customer service. Seeking to make a difference, Anna turned to ChatGPT in search of an innovative solution; using her skills in software development and artificial intelligence (AI), Anna designed an app designed to automate customer service for small businesses.

Anna used ChatGPT's capabilities to design an intelligent app that was both user-friendly and intelligent, using artificial intelligence (AI) for routine inquiries to provide fast, accurate responses that reduced human customer service representative workload significantly.

This app's power lies in its capacity to learn and adapt from interactions, constantly adapting its responses and interactions to meet the unique requirements of small businesses. Created specifically to understand and meet those of entrepreneurs juggling multiple roles simultaneously.

Anna's app quickly gained the favor of small business owners upon its debut due to its affordability and efficiency in handling customer interactions - both factors which are integral for running on tight budgets. Business owners appreciated how Anna's app freed them up time so they could focus more directly on other aspects of their operations.

Anna's success with ChatGPT shows its potential as an innovative solution that meets market needs. Not only has her innovation revolutionized small business community but has also established Anna as an authority on using AI technology to solve real world business issues.

14. ChatGPT for Market Research and Analysis

Understanding market trends and consumer behavior are critical components of business. ChatGPT can assist businesses by collecting and analyzing market data to provide insights that will shape strategies and decisions made within them.

Padronzo, an innovative market analyst, leveraged AI technology to transform his approach to market research and analysis. His role required sifting through vast amounts of market data and consumer trends to provide his clients with actionable insights - ChatGPT became his go-to tool, helping him dive deep into market dynamics with unprecedented efficiency.

Padronzo leveraged ChatGPT's prompts such as, "Analyze consumer trends for [industry]" and "Summarize market research findings on [product or service]," to quickly interpret complex datasets. His approach allowed him to quickly identify emerging patterns or market shifts that may otherwise go undetected.

AI's ability to analyze large volumes of data quickly and present findings clearly was revolutionary for Padronzo's workload; allowing him to focus more on strategic analysis than data processing. His reports featuring AI-generated insights provided clients with greater insights into their markets and consumers.

ChatGPT provided Padronzo's clients with accurate, data-driven analysis that allowed them to make informed, informed decisions -

identifying new opportunities and tailoring marketing strategies accordingly; thus becoming an indispensable analyst within his field. His ability quickly made him one of the go-to analysts in his area.

Padronzo's story illustrates the revolutionary potential of AI technology in market research. By employing ChatGPT, he was not only able to enhance his analytical abilities but also add significant value to client services - strengthening his position as a leading market analyst.

15. Scaling Business Operations with ChatGPT

Management of operations becomes more complicated as businesses expand. ChatGPT can assist businesses by streamlining inventory control and logistics operations to make scaling up easier on both themselves and resources.

Nano, an ambitious e-commerce entrepreneur, recognized the need to optimize her inventory and logistics as her platform grew. Her challenge lay in scaling her operations efficiently without needing more staff or resources; ChatGPT provided her with the solution she needed, revolutionizing how she approached managing inventory and logistics.

Nano began using ChatGPT to automate various aspects of her inventory management. She would set up prompts like: "Generate weekly inventory reports for [product category]" and "Alert on low stock levels for [specific items]." This allowed her to maintain optimal stock levels without overstock or stockout issues - both costly situations in an e-commerce business.

ChatGPT enabled her to use its features to optimize her logistics more effectively, prompting her to "Optimize shipping routes for orders from [region]" and "Create a schedule for restocking based on sales forecasts". As a result, Nano was able to make her logistics more effective, leading to faster delivery times with lower shipping costs as well as increasing customer satisfaction.

One of the greatest advantages of ChatGPT for Melissa was its seamless scaling capabilities. As her e-commerce platform expanded, ChatGPT handled its increasing complexity of inventory and logistics management without needing to hire additional team members, substantially cutting operational costs in half.

Nano's successful use of ChatGPT to manage her e-commerce platform's inventory and logistics is testament to AI's transformative potential in business processes. By adopting AI solutions such as ChatGPT for inventory and logistics management, she was able to scale her business efficiently while remaining lean, as well as focus on strategic growth areas - her story serves as an inspiration to any e-commerce entrepreneurs looking for innovative technologies for business expansion.

Conclusion - ChatGPT provides many opportunities for monetizing services and expanding businesses, and mastering its use can open up an abundance of income-generation and expansion possibilities for your business or service model. By harnessing AI through Chat GPT Millionaire Goldmine you will unlock an abundance of new possibilities - be they freelancer, entrepreneur or business owner alike this guide serves as your road to AI-fueled success!

CHAPTER 10

LOOKING TO THE HORIZON: MULTIPLY YOUR INCOME WITH FUTURE INNOVATIONS IN AI

Let me walk you through my story - the story of how Austin Welch, an enthusiast in digital marketing and e-commerce, became one of the pioneers in using artificial intelligence to revolutionize online marketing and business.

My journey started over a decade ago in a small studio full of ideas and ambition. I was always enthralled with digital marketing and e-commerce, testing various business models and creating brands with lasting impressions on consumers. More than just participating, though; I wanted to redefine it; from day one, my focus wasn't simply to offer products or services; rather it was on creating experiences for customers that resonated deeply with them - something which transcends merely selling products or services.

Over the years I've attempted to stay informed on emerging technologies and met with various tech company founders to understand their new creations. When I came across ChatGPT I knew it would change everything for me. At first it seemed like just another tool in my toolbox, but soon enough it opened up an entirely new realm of possibility.

Soon enough, I realized AI was more than a toy to ask mundane questions of. So, I began experimenting with ChatGPT as part of my digital marketing strategies and company structures, using our protagonists Emma and Lucas to show you. Through AI I adapted campaigns to target specific customers while producing creative content efficiently; my efficiency improved as costs decreased while elevating customer experiences to an entirely new level! The results were simply remarkable! Not only was the customer experience improved considerably while costs decreased drastically but customer retention rates also saw dramatic gains!

As part of my passion to share knowledge and expertise with the world, I decided to offer an online course on using ChatGPT in digital marketing and e-commerce. From basic AI theory to its application in different aspects of online business, the course was an overwhelming success and attracted students from around the globe while becoming an excellent source of passive income.

My income from the course enabled me to diversify my investments, including partnerships with startups, advice to companies, and AI-based solutions for various industries. Each project served as an opportunity to learn and expand my understanding of how AI could transform businesses of various sizes across sectors.

One of the key lessons I gained on my journey was about adaptability. Technology advances rapidly; to stay abreast of changes requires being open-minded, quick to pick up new information quickly and capable of quickly adapting to changes as they come along.

Still, I remain optimistic about digital marketing and e-commerce being closely tied with AI in future. In my vision of it all, advanced personalization, intelligent automation, predictive analytics will all become mainstream technologies; for those willing to embrace them the possibilities are truly endless.

My story is one of passion, curiosity and constant innovation - an amazing journey filled with challenges and rewards. In this book, I aim to encourage you to explore ChatGPT and AI; whether you're an aspiring entrepreneur, marketing professional or simply curious about technology's endless potential, join me as I embark on this exciting voyage into a future filled with limitless potential!

Innovation is the driving force of change in this ever-evolving digital sphere, so having access to the necessary tools and an open attitude are keys to making your dreams a reality. So as you wrap up this book, remember that every ending marks only the start of something new; just take time out of each day to explore and seize opportunities presented before you.

My story goes beyond ChatGPT or artificial intelligence; it's about innovation and entrepreneurship. Each product, marketing campaign, strategy implementation strategy and piece of content I produced were not just tasks on my to-do list; rather they represented opportunities to explore and push boundaries of digital possibilities.

My digital transformation journey was an essential one. Not just adopting new technologies, but recognizing their ability to enhance every facet of my business from customer experience optimization to automating internal processes was essential in creating an efficient and profitable enterprise.

ChatGPT quickly became more than a tool; it became an indispensable business partner. AI-generated text not only saved me both time and resources, but it also opened new channels of engagement with my target audience that had previously been impossible.

My journey wasn't without obstacles though! There were moments of doubt where strategies failed to come together as expected or results did not match what had been envisioned; yet every obstacle presented an opportunity for growth and learning; perseverance, an openness to experimentation and being quick at adapting quickly were essential in surmounting them successfully. As I discussed in this book and as one of my key recommendations, a central aspect of my success has been building my knowledge network. Collaborating with other professionals, participating in forums and communities, and maintaining regular dialogues with experts from e-commerce, AI, digital marketing were crucial components to my growth as an AI marketing professional. Learning together and collaboration were both integral parts of success; no one is an island in this arena!

Looking ahead, I anticipate an increasingly level playing field, where small businesses and entrepreneurs can compete effectively with large corporations using tools such as ChatGPT. In order to remain ahead, success requires adapting quickly to new technologies and trends as well as being open-minded when trying out innovative approaches.

My story from humble beginnings to where it stands today is an inspirational tale that shows what can happen when passion meets technology. ChatGPT proved more than a tool; it helped propel my business to new heights and reach success I never could have predicted. Anyone can find their own path to digital age success with an open mind, willingness to learn and adapt, experimentation and innovation - the future is full of opportunities waiting to be discovered on our journey towards it all!

As I look back over my journey, it is apparent that digital business and then its integration and improvement through ChatGPT was an integral component in both my professional career and personal life. ChatGPT allowed me to break free from traditional 9 to 5 jobs while attaining financial independence previously unthinkable.

Traditional 9-to-5 jobs often limit creativity and entrepreneurialism. Launching my own digital business opened up a whole world of opportunity: no longer tied down to desk or schedule constraints allowed me to work from any location at any time for maximum creativity and efficiency in daily activities.

ChatGPT is more than a tool to streamline existing processes; it's a catalyst to creating innovative business models and revenue opportunities. I discovered ChatGPT when using it to produce high-quality blog content - which became an income stream after just dedicating a small number of hours per month to it! Incorporating ChatGPT into social media management allowed me to provide more efficient digital marketing services and increase clientele base exponentially.

ChatGPT's versatility opens a host of business models. From creating online courses and eBooks to building custom AI tools for other businesses, the possibilities are vast. From my own experience, the key to ChatGPT success has been finding applications that solve real world issues.

Digital technology presents us with many opportunities. If you're seeking to start their own business, expand an existing one, or simply explore alternative income streams - ChatGPT can provide an effective route towards realizing those goals.

Over time, I have come to appreciate that what has brought me the greatest satisfaction is not financial independence but rather the freedom to follow my passions and live my life according to my own terms. ChatGPT provided my entryway into an exciting future of creativity, innovation and technology coming together for unparalleled opportunities.

Now I want to turn my attention toward you, the reader. ChatGPT stands at the edge of an exciting digital universe of unbound possibilities; I urge you to take the first steps on your personal transformation journey today - whether that means leaving behind 9-to-5 grind, diversifying income streams or exploring creative outlets, ChatGPT can help get there faster than ever!

Start small by developing an easily executable business model using ChatGPT. From marketing services and customer care to content creation or any other area that inspires you - every journey begins with small steps.

At the forefront of an AI revolution lies ChatGPT: an AI that is revolutionizing how financial services work for you and is revolutionizing financial independence, freedom and success for many - don't get left behind; take this chance to be part of it! Financial independence, freedom and success await - ChatGPT can help guide your path on this exciting path!

If this book has inspired or provided valuable information for you, or helped to kick-start your exploration and implementation of ChatGPT, I would greatly appreciate if you could leave an Amazon review with your thoughts and feedback. It can not only assist me as an author but may be the beacon that guides others toward discovery and success with ChatGPT.

As you close this book, remember that your future is something you are shaping now. ChatGPT is more than a tool; it is the gateway to a future in which your full potential can be realized. Thank you for joining me on my journey through "ChatGPT Goldmine", I hope this marks just the start of your own success and transformation story - take that first step, experiment, explore, experimentation and transform yourself - AI awaits!

BONUS CHAPTER I: ETHICAL AND SAFE BROWSING IN MONETIZATION WITH CHATGPT

In this digital journey towards monetization with the help of artificial intelligence, it is crucial to address a vitally important issue: ethics and security in the use of tools such as ChatGPT. In this chapter, we will explore how to strike a balance between generating revenue and maintaining ethical and transparent conduct, while ensuring the protection of our brand.

The Balance between Income and Ethics

As our initial step, our aim is to understand and address ethical challenges associated with AI monetization.

As AI continues its advancements, ethical concerns can arise concerning data privacy and authenticity of generated content. When collecting user data via ChatGPT, for instance, transparency regarding how that data will be utilized must be ensured - one approach would be adding a prompt in ChatGPT that informs users about this use via prompts like: "Generate an informative message that informs our users on how we collect and utilize user data securely and ethically to improve services".

Trust is of great value in digital society. In order to build it effectively and establish yourself as a respected brand, AI use must be ethical and transparent. When using ChatGPT as part of blog content generation, add an explanation that its assistance was AI assisted, thus maintaining honest communications with your readers. Being forthcoming about how ChatGPT helps your services or products such as product descriptions on websites if applicable could also contribute to customer trust building - perhaps by including an indication that ChatGPT assisted.

AI can have both ethical and legal ramifications when implemented properly, such as data privacy regulations in your region and copyright legislation for third party content generation services like ChatGPT; always verifying originality before creating content through ChatGPT to avoid violating other's copyright rights.

Adopting and following ethical principles and best practices are absolutely critical in AI-enabled environments, including respecting users' privacy, being open about AI usage and producing legal, compliant content. You can use ChatGPT to stay abreast of best practices related to AI ethics by asking it for updates about current trends or recommendations in this space, although for optimal results I suggest consulting professional. AI world evolves quickly - make sure you stay abreast!

Ensuring Transparent and Authentic Communication, Protecting your Brand

Part two of our journey entails upholding authenticity and protecting the brand in an AI-led world.

Artificial Intelligence, particularly ChatGPT, can be an invaluable asset when it comes to cultivating and protecting your online reputation. ChatGPT makes this possible by monitoring brand mentions across social media and creating appropriate responses based on ethical considerations to user comments - for example by monitoring recent mentions that reflect company values or commitment to quality". A good prompt for use might be: "Please analyze recent mentions of our brand on social media to generate responses reflecting company values".

Artificial Intelligence can assist content creation, yet humanizing it remains essential to maintaining authenticity. One approach would be combining AI-generated articles with your personal insights or experiences for more authenticity; ChatGPT could generate draft articles but you should add personalization by sharing stories or insights of your own to add authenticity.

On the flipside, using AI in business may also attract criticism; when concerns are voiced directly address them and demonstrate how ChatGPT operates ethically and responsibly.

Protecting both your business and brand requires safeguarding all digital tools used. Implement strong security protocols when protecting ChatGPT data as well as other systems. Furthermore, stay current on software upgrades while employing recommended protection tools like firewalls and antivirus programs to maintain maximum protection of both.

Education is of vital importance in this rapidly-evolving digital landscape, so staying informed on recent AI trends and digital ethics developments is imperative. ChatGPT offers educational resources such as webinars or courses to keep your skills and knowledge current.

Navigating ethical and safe monetization using ChatGPT requires striking a delicate yet essential balance. Adopting a strategy which prioritizes transparency, authenticity and ethics will not only protect your brand but also foster relationships of trust with audiences. This chapter has provided you with all of the tools and knowledge to face these challenges head on and leverage AI opportunities effectively for sustainable, responsible digital success.

On our journey towards ethical and secure monetization with ChatGPT, let's examine how the case studies in this book can be modified in order to maintain ethics while protecting brand assets - adaptions that readers will immediately implement into actionable steps that they will find beneficial and implementable solutions immediately.

Responsible Use of Chatbots and Ethical Data Management

Chatbots, powered by technologies such as ChatGPT, are powerful tools for improving customer interaction. However, their responsible use is crucial. Make sure your chatbot clearly informs users that they are interacting with an AI and not a human. A practical example of a prompt would be: "Design an initial message for our chatbot that clearly states that it is an AI and explains how it can assist users".

As part of your interactions with customers, you may come into contact with sensitive data that requires special care and consideration when collecting it. It is vital that any collected information be handled with due regard for privacy; you should consider adding a Privacy Policy page on your website that accommodates for national legislation governing each user whose data may be collected.

Transparent Communication in Digital Marketing

Digital marketing depends on transparency of communication. When using ChatGPT to generate promotional or advertising content, make sure it accurately represents your products or services. A useful prompt might be: "Generate an advertising campaign for our new product that showcases its real features and benefits without exaggeration".

At a time of widespread misinformation, it is critical that AI-generated information be accurate and truthful. When using ChatGPT to generate informational content, be sure to regularly verify its accuracy by telling the AI what sources constitute reliable sources or what not. You could say, for instance: "Verify accuracy of nutrition article." To be more specific, provide feedback or training the AI on what constitutes reliable sources versus unreliable ones.

Launch an open dialogue with your audience regarding why and how ChatGPT is being utilized, to help foster trust and respect between yourselves. Hold Q&A sessions or webinars that explore the integration of AI in your services or products.

Consider engaging AI ethics experts to review and enhance your practices, offering invaluable advice while ensuring they adhere to ethical best practices. ChatGPT allows you to quickly locate leading experts in this area as well as plan how best to approach them: "Create a list of AI ethics experts and propose a plan to collaborate with them in reviewing our practices".

Content Generation Responsibility

As part of your content generation in ChatGPT, it is your responsibility to ensure it is respectful and non-offensive. This requires being mindful of sensitive topics as well as not creating material which may be perceived as discriminatory or harmful. As an example prompt would suggest: "Review this generated content to ensure it is inclusive while revising any parts which may pose problems".

As part of your use of ChatGPT, it is crucial that you respect the intellectual property rights of others. This includes not generating content which infringes upon copyrights or trademarks. A practical prompt might include something like this: "Generate original content for our blog that does not infringe any intellectual property and offers unique value to readers". Furthermore, anti-plagiarism tools may help in this respect.

Staying current on any changes to AI regulations that could impede its use is paramount to successful AI business practices, including ChatGPT and other AI systems. An effective prompt would be: "Provide an up-to-date summary of AI regulations and standards which could impact our business, especially regarding data privacy and copyright."

One proactive step that many companies have already taken is forming an internal ethics committee dedicated to overseeing your use of AI. This committee should stay abreast of emerging AI ethics trends and debates and ensure your practices conform with industry standards. If you work solo or run a small company, try spending one or two hours every week keeping yourself abreast of best practices related to AI as an individual ethics committee member yourself.

Consider conducting regular audits of your AI practices and systems, in order to make sure they continue to comply with ethical and legal practices. Audits might include reviewing ChatGPT data generated and how it's being utilized - for instance a prompt for this exercise may include "Design a checklist that assesses compliance with ethical and legal practices".

Promoting a Culture of Digital Responsibility

AI ethics awareness and training should not only be for business leaders, but also for all employees. Use ChatGPT to develop training materials and awareness programs that help your team understand the importance of AI ethics. A prompt might be, "Create an employee training program on AI ethics, including case studies and best practices."

In advertising and marketing, the use of AI must be not only efficient, but also ethical. Make sure that any AI-generated content for these areas is honest and not misleading. You can create an advertising campaign with the message that your brand does use AI responsibly.

Finally, foster a culture of digital responsibility in your organization. This means going beyond just complying with regulations and truly embracing ethics as a core value.

Conclusion: A Commitment to Ethical Excellence

At the conclusion of this chapter, my goal is that you will gain a profound appreciation for ethics and security when using ChatGPT to monetize. Technology such as AI can offer incredible opportunities to develop in digital environments; it is our duty to use such tools responsibly by respecting individual dignity, rights and protecting brand integrity.

Ethics are both moral and practical considerations when using AI; adopting ethical practices builds both an enduring business and reputational advantage for companies that prioritize ethical approaches. Companies that prioritize ethics earn customer and social trust.

As AI continues to develop, so too will its ethical and legal considerations. Being at the forefront of these conversations and practices is not only necessary but can serve as an opportunity to lead in an area that will shape both business and society in years to come.

An essential practice in ethical AI use is conducting regular audits. Audits go beyond simple review; they involve an in-depth and critical examination of how tools like ChatGPT are being utilized within your business and should examine both compliance with current laws as well as how your practices align with evolving ethical standards.

An audit might start by looking at what data ChatGPT is processing - such as personal and sensitive information? How is this being protected? Additionally, the audit should evaluate how ChatGPT outputs are being utilized; such as are they being used to create misleading or manipulative content or checked and corrected manually to maintain high quality and accuracy?

Marketing and advertising rely heavily on AI technology, making its ethical use essential. Here, the line between persuasion and manipulation can often be tenuous; thus it is imperative that companies adhere to practices that respect customers' autonomy and intelligence.

As part of ChatGPT's use for digital marketing content creation, it is critical that we ask ourselves whether this content accurately represents our product or service? Are we exaggerating or making promises our product cannot keep? An ethical approach to digital marketing not only protects consumers but also builds long-term brand credibility and trust with consumers.

Transparency is both ethical and strategic in the digital realm; consumers today value brands that are transparent about their practices; being forthcoming about your use of AI can become an asset in selling out your campaigns.

Fostering a culture of digital responsibility goes far beyond policies and audits; it involves instilling values throughout your organization that ensure every employee, from CEO to entry level staffer, understands the ethical considerations inherent to AI use.

Promoting an atmosphere of transparency and openness is also paramount, creating an environment in which employees feel comfortable voicing any queries about how AI is being utilized. A culture which prizes ethics and accountability ensures employees understand their role in upholding such standards.

By all accounts, ethical and safe monetization with ChatGPT involves more than just adhering to rules; it involves making a commitment to ethical excellence that builds an iconic brand known for both financial success and integrity.

As we close this chapter, I encourage you to think about how these practices can apply in your use of AI. Every decision made regarding technologies like ChatGPT affects not only your business but also contributes to how AI shapes the world. By prioritizing ethics, transparency, and accountability in your technology usage choices, you are opting for a future where tech advances our businesses while simultaneously upholding humanity and values.

At this juncture in technology and business ethics history, it is crucial that we acknowledge we are at a pivotal juncture. How we choose to utilize tools like ChatGPT will not only influence immediate business success but will also shape future generations of technologies and businesses operating under similar ethical frameworks.

AI will undoubtedly play a transformative role in all areas of life and work. With this technological development comes an inescapable responsibility: we must ensure that advancement does not come at the cost of ethical principles; instead of seeing ethics as something restrictive or hindering innovation, they should be seen as the path toward genuine progress and genuine innovation.

Empathy and social awareness should be at the core of our interactions with emerging technologies like ChatGPT. When developing and using technologies such as this one, it is imperative to consider not only its financial implications but also how its use impacts individuals and society at large - this requires conscious efforts at understanding and addressing ethical concerns from data protection to fairness in AI applications.

As leaders, entrepreneurs, and creators in the digital era, we have an opportunity to lead by example in setting ethical values as part of innovation processes and commercial success. Our commitment to responsible innovation not only strengthens our own integrity as business entities but also encourages others to follow a similar path.

In the following chapters, we will continue exploring how best to leverage tools such as ChatGPT while taking care to foster responsibility, innovation and respect for core values that unite us as global citizens. Working together we can work toward an improved world where technology and ethics coexist harmoniously - one which is both more advanced but also more equitable, inclusive and humane.

BONUS CHAPTER II: GPT CHAT NOVEMBER 2023 UPDATE - GPT CHAT 4 TURBO: CREATING AND MONETIZING GPTS

Like Austin Welch, I've had a first-hand experience of the exciting development of ChatGPT and now, with the arrival of Chat GPT 4 Turbo, we are facing a new era: that of creating and marketing personalized GPTs. The November 2023 update is not only a technical upgrade, but also a revolution in how we interact with and monetize artificial intelligence.

Chat GPT 4 Turbo marks a milestone in the evolution of generative language models. With improvements in speed, accuracy and personalization, this tool opens new paths for entrepreneurship and digital innovation.

Let's imagine a GPT called "Fitness Mentor AI". This model is designed for personal trainers and fitness enthusiasts, incorporating advanced knowledge in nutrition, exercise routines and wellness tips.

1. **Knowledge Base Building**: We integrate nutrition guides, personalized exercise routines and general wellness tips.
2. **Interaction Programming**: "Fitness Mentor AI" is designed to interact with users, providing personalized recommendations and adjustments to their workout routines.

3. **Practical Application**: This GPT becomes an invaluable tool for gyms and personal trainers, offering a personalized consultation and training service.

With the opening of the OpenAI GPT Store, you can sell your customized GPT, as a "Fitness Mentor AI", to a specific market, generating revenue through its practical application in the fitness and wellness sector.

1. **Target Market Definition**: Identify a niche that would benefit from your GPT, such as gyms, personal trainers or fitness apps.
2. **Marketing and Sales**: Promote your GPT using digital marketing strategies, highlighting its unique value and specific benefits.
3. **Business Models and Pricing**: Decide how you will monetize your GPT. You can opt for direct sales, subscriptions or pay-per-use models.

GPT-4 Turbo stands as a new frontier of AI, producing richer and more relevant content generation than before. This upgrade opens up endless opportunities in many fields--ranging from fitness to education--across multiple applications.

OpenAI has taken measures to provide legal protection to GPT users, an important consideration when creating potentially copyrighted material. As creators and creators, we should all be mindful of any regulations that exist to help safeguard our work as well as our users.

Custom GPT creation and commercialization opens a whole new era in artificial intelligence (AI), giving us the chance to lead this technological breakthrough forward. From Fitness Mentor AI-type

GPTs for niche markets like gyms to investigating other fields with similar problems - there is so much potential here! We look forward to being at the forefront of innovation.

I urge you to embark on this exciting and fulfilling adventure of creating and commercializing your GPT. By applying creativity, skill, and a clear understanding of your target market you can turn this technology into both income and personal satisfaction - AI is shaping our world, and now is your opportunity to help shape its development!

BONUS CHAPTER III: DIRECTORY OF AI TOOLS AND INTEGRATION STRATEGIES BY APPLICATION AREAS

This chapter offers practical guidance to those looking to leverage AI into their business strategies. AI encompasses an expansive universe filled with innovative tools designed to transform various areas of your organization - beyond ChatGPT alone! Here, we explore an exhaustive directory of these tools in depth; exploring each one in detail to integrate and maximize them effectively for optimal use in various business sectors. To achieve superior results using multiple tools simultaneously. I introduce you to several AI tools with their respective applications so you can maximize their potential while increasing results across sectors. When combined together for maximum effect - here.

My experience shows that ChatGPT is an invaluable asset, but its effectiveness increases exponentially when coupled with other AI solutions.

At the core of every successful AI strategy is a smart integration of different tools. When working on marketing campaigns, I typically start with Jasper AI to gather a base level of content before using ChatGPT to add humanization and ensure alignment with brand voice. Finally, Canva AI provides engaging graphics to complement text.

Practical Strategies for Integration

1. Needs Analysis: Before selecting AI tools, carefully evaluate your needs and goals. For example, if your focus is on content marketing, a combination of ChatGPT, Jasper AI and Canva may be ideal.
2. Testing and Adjusting: Experiment with different combinations of tools and adjust your strategy according to the results. Observe how each tool affects overall performance and make adjustments as necessary.
3. Continuing Education: Stay current on the latest trends and updates in AI tools. Attending webinars, online courses and conferences is essential to understand how to maximize the potential of these technologies.
4. Ongoing Evaluation: Regularly monitor the performance of your AI strategies. Use metrics and feedback to evaluate the effectiveness of your tool combinations and make adjustments when necessary.

A Practical Guide to Choosing the Right Tools

1. **Identify your Objectives**: Clearly define what you want to achieve with AI. Are you looking to improve efficiency, increase engagement, or something different?
2. **Research and Compare**: Research each tool, its capabilities and how they compare to each other. Look for reviews, case studies and testimonials to get a comprehensive view.
3. **Free Trial and Demos**: Most AI tools offer trial versions or demos. Use them to gain first-hand experience before making a purchasing decision.

4. **Consider Integration and Compatibility**: Make sure the tools you choose can easily integrate with one another as well as with existing systems.
5. **Support and Community**: An AI solution with strong customer support and an active community can be invaluable when beginning to integrate AI into operations.

Once again, depending on which areas you want to cover:

Digital Marketing and Advertising

- **ChatGPT**: Content generation and customer service.
- **Jasper AI**: Creation of ad drafts and copywriting.
- **Canva AI**: Graphic and visual design.
- **Adext AI**: Digital advertising automation.
- **Albert AI**: Optimization of advertising campaigns.

2. Customer Service and CRM

- **Zendesk AI**: Automated support and ticket management.
- **Salesforce Einstein**: CRM data analysis and forecasting.
- **Drift AI**: Chatbots for sales and customer service.
- **Intercom AI**: Personalized messaging and conversation management.

Content Generation and SEO

- **SEMRush Writing Assistant**: Content optimization for SEO.
- **Grammarly AI**: Improving text quality and grammar.
- **MarketMuse**: Content planning and SEO strategy.
- **Frase AI**: Content research and automatic article generation.

4. Data Analysis and Business Intelligence

- **Tableau AI**: Data visualization and analysis.
- **MonkeyLearn AI**: Text analysis and data extraction.
- **Databricks**: AI-based analysis platform.
- **Google AI Platform**: Predictive analytics and machine learning.

5. Product and Service Development

- **Azure AI**: AI application development tools.
- **IBM Watson Studio**: Building and training AI models.
- **Aible**: Creation of business-specific AI models.
- **BigML**: Creation of predictive models and classifiers.

6. Education and Training

- **Coursera AI**: Courses and certifications in AI.
- **EdX AI**: Educational programs in artificial intelligence.
- **Duolingo AI**: AI-assisted language learning.
- **Socratic by Google**: Helps with learning and solving tasks.

7. E-commerce and Online Sales

- **Algolia AI**: AI-driven search and discovery.
- **Klevu AI**: Intelligent search engine for online stores.
- **Recombee AI**: Personalized product recommendations.
- **Sentient Ascend AI**: Real-time conversion optimization.

At each application area, selecting and combining tools that best complement one another to maximize their potential is of utmost importance. For example, in digital marketing the combination of ChatGPT for content production, Adext AI for ad automation, SEMRush for SEO monitoring and SEMRush's ranking tool SEMRush can make for a comprehensive strategy; and for data analytics Tableau can provide visualization while MonkeyLearn text analytics and Google AI Platform predictive analytics provide deeper, actionable insights for your business.

An intelligent integration of multiple AI tools can bring many benefits to any business, from marketing and customer service to data analytics and product development. I encourage you to explore these tools, experiment with combinations, and find those which best suit your company needs - AI can become an indispensable asset to help drive its expansion and success!

Embarking on the AI Innovation Journey

As I come to an end with "ChatGPT Goldmine," it's worth pausing to consider our journey together. From learning ChatGPT's capabilities and exploring advanced AI tools to witnessing ChatGPT evolve over time and expand with AI tools available today - my aim was not just to show tools available; rather I hoped to empower and inspire readers with innovative thinking about how AI could transform business operations and lives alike - real "gold mine" of ChatGPT lies in its capacity to free us from conventional constraints while opening new opportunities that help connect and serve customers and communities alike!

Now is your turn to embark upon this incredible journey of innovation and change! Equipped with tools and knowledge gained thus far, each one of you has the power to forge a future where technology and humanity interweave seamlessly, enriching our lives and businesses alike. I encourage you to view this book not as the end, but as just the start of an incredible AI adventure - experiment, explore and don't be scared to take calculated risks; remember this era offers vast opportunity! Let this book serve as your springboard into AI; prepare yourselves - the future awaits!

DISCLAIMER

This book is written and provided for educational and informational purposes only. The contents of this book are not intended to offer personal, financial, legal, or professional advice. While the information contained within the book is periodically updated and based on research, the rapidly evolving nature of AI technology and financial markets means that no guarantee is given regarding the accuracy, relevance, timeliness, or completeness of any information presented.

The author and publisher of this book disclaim any liabilities or losses incurred as a direct or indirect result of the application of any information presented herein. This book is not a substitute for professional financial or legal consultation; therefore, the reader is strongly encouraged to consult with professional advisors for advice tailored to their specific circumstances.

The use of the information in this book is solely at the reader's risk. The author and publisher do not warrant that any monetary success or profit will result from the application of the information provided. Additionally, the author and publisher shall not be responsible for any errors or omissions in this book or for the availability of this information.

By reading this book, you agree that under no circumstances will the author and publisher be liable for any direct, indirect, incidental, consequential, special, or exemplary damages arising out of or in connection with the use of the information provided in this book.

Made in the USA
Monee, IL
04 November 2026

67377511R00075